ESTATE PUBLICATIONS

DERBY

C000077621

Street maps with index
Administrative Districts
Population Gazetteer
Road Map with index
Postcodes

Street plans prepared and published by ESTATE PUBLICATIONS, Bridewell House, TENTERDEN, KENT, and based upon the ORDNANCE SURVEY mapping with the permission of the Controller of H. M. Stationery Office.

The Publishers acknowledge the co-operation of the local authorities of towns represented in this atlas.

COUNTY RED BOOK

DERBYSHIRE

contains street maps for each town centre

SUPER & LOCAL RED BOOKS

are street atlases with comprehensive local coverage

ALFRETON & BELPER

including: Heanor, Matlock,
Matlock Bath, Ripley, Wirksworth etc.

DERBY

including: Borrowash, Chellaston,
Duffield, Heanor, Mickleover,
Spondon etc.

BURTON UPON TRENT

including: Ashby-de-la-Zouch,
Barton-under-Needwood, Linton,
Repton, Swadlincote, Tutbury etc.

MANSFIELD

including: Bolsover, Kirkby in Ashfield,
Mansfield Woodhouse,
Sutton in Ashfield etc.

CHESTERFIELD

including: Clay Cross, Dronfield,
Staveley etc.

NOTTINGHAM

including: Arnold, Carlton, Eastwood,
Hucknall, Ilkeston, Kirk Hallam,
Long Eaton etc.

CONTENTS

LEGEND TO STREET MAPS

One-Way Street	→	Post Office	●
Pedestrianized	▨	Public Convenience	Ⓒ
Car Park	Ⓟ	Place of Worship	+

Scale of street plans: 4 Inches to 1 mile (unless otherwise stated on the map).

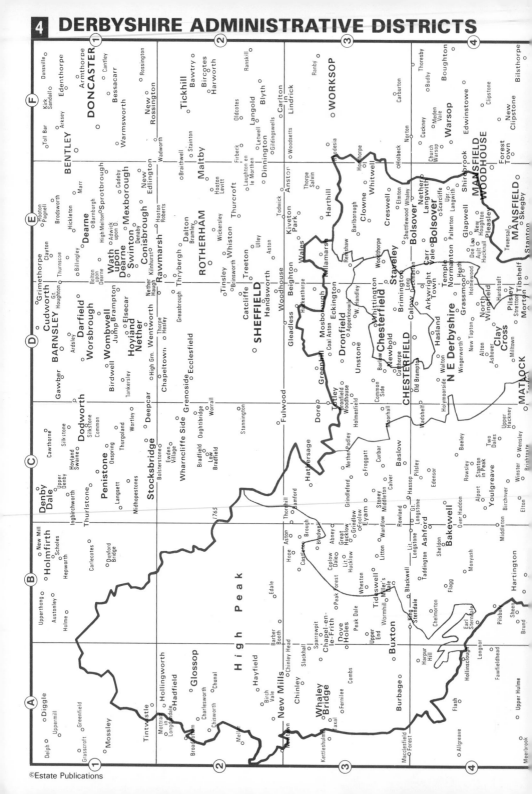

4 DERBYSHIRE ADMINISTRATIVE DISTRICTS

©Estate Publications

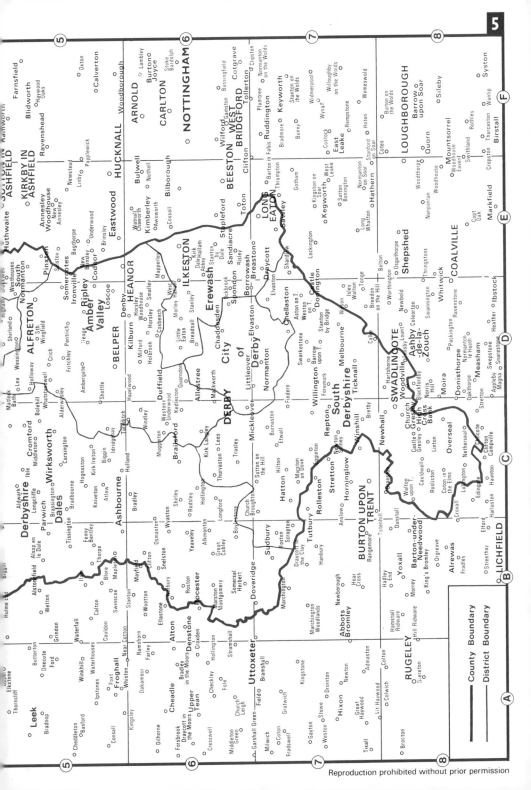

GAZETTEER INDEX TO ROAD MAP
with Populations

County of Derbyshire population **928,636**

Districts:

Amber Valley	111,897
Bolsover	70,437
Chesterfield	99,403
Derby	218,802
Derbyshire Dales	67,562
Erewash	106,101
High Peak	85,092
North East Derbyshire	97,570
South Derbyshire	71,772

Abney & Abney Grange 52	8 C4	
Aldercar &		
Langley Mill 4,951	*	
Alderwasley 368	11 E1	
Aldwark 33	10 C1	
Alfreton 8,276	11 E1	
Alkmonton 68	10 C3	
Allestree	11 E3	
Alport	8 C6	
Alsop en la Dale	10 C1	
Alton	9 E6	
Ambergate	11 E2	
Apperknowle	9 E4	
Arkwright Town	9 F5	
Ash 63	*	
Ashbourne 6,300	10 C2	
Ashford in the Water 525	8 C5	
Ashleyhay 110	*	
Ashover 1,776	9 E6	
Aston 100	8 C4	
Aston upon Trent 1,603	11 E4	
Atlow 89	10 C2	
Ault Hucknall 850	*	
Bakewell 3,818	8 C6	
Ballidon 76	*	
Bamford 1,089	8 C4	
Barber Booth	8 B3	
Barlborough 1,917	9 F4	
Barlow 957	9 E5	
Barrow upon Trent 529	11 E4	
Barton Blount 55	*	
Baslow & Bubnell 1,184	8 D5	
Bearwardcote 33	*	
Beeley 190	8 D6	
Belper 16,960	11 E2	
Biggin 103	10 C1	
Biggin	10 D2	
Birch Vale	8 A3	
Birchover 332	8 C6	
Blackwell in the Peak 30	8 B5	
Blackwell 4,194	*	
Boldhill	10 D1	
Bolsover 11,232	9 F5	
Bonsall 807	*	
Borrowash	11 F4	
Boylestone 154	10 C3	
Brackenfield 200	11 E1	
Bradbourne 112	10 C1	
Bradley 265	10 C2	
Bradwell 1,426	8 C4	
Brailsford 836	10 D3	
Brampton 1,221	9 E5	
Brassington 535	10 C1	

Breadsall 816	11 E3	
Breaston 4,502	11 F4	
Bretby 783	10 D5	
Brightgate	10 D1	
Brimington 8,560	9 E5	
Brough & Shatton 144	8 C4	
Brushfield 15	*	
Burbage	8 A5	
Burnaston 553	10 D4	
Buxton 20,380	8 B5	
Calke 26	11 E5	
Callow 44	*	
Calow 2,557	9 E5	
Calver 723	8 D5	
Carr Vale	9 F5	
Carsington 111	10 D1	
Castle Gresley 1,516	10 D6	
Castleton 689	8 C4	
Catton 61	*	
Cauldwell 124	10 D6	
Chaddesden	11 E3	
Chapel-en-le-Frith 8,507	8 B4	
Charlesworth 2,140	8 A3	
Chatsworth 60	*	
Chellaston	11 E4	
Chelmorton 317	8 B5	
Chesterfield 74,299	9 E5	
Chinley, Buxworth &		
Brownside 2,391	8 A4	
Chinley Head	8 B4	
Chisworth 244	8 A3	
Chunal	8 A3	
Church Broughton 483	10 C4	
Church Gresley	10 D6	
Clay Cross 8,749	9 E6	
Clifton & Compton 444	10 C2	
Clowne 7,234	9 F5	
Coal Aston	9 E4	
Codnor 4,070	11 F2	
Combs	8 A4	
Common Side	9 E5	
Coplow Dale	8 C4	
Coton in the Elms 782	10 D6	
Coxbench	11 E2	
Creswell	9 G5	
Crich 2,820	11 E1	
Cromford 1,669	10 D1	
Cubley 222	10 C3	
Curbar 431	8 D5	
Cutthorpe	9 E5	
Dalbury Lees 186	*	
Dale Abbey 1,571	11 F3	
Darley Dale 4,764	*	
Denby 1,875	11 E2	
Derby 218,802	11 E3	
Derwent 44	*	
Dethick Lea &		
Holloway 1,136	11 E1	
Doe Lea	9 F6	
Doveridge 1,249	10 B4	
Doves Holes	8 B4	
Drakelow 123	*	
Draycott &		
Church Wilne 2,782	11 F4	

Dronfield 22,985	9 E4	
Dronfield Woodhouse	8 D4	
Duffield 4,514	11 E3	
Earl Sterndale	8 B6	
Eaton & Alsop 89	*	
Eckington 10,854	9 E4	
Edale 350	8 B3	
Edensore 180	8 D5	
Edlaston & Wyaston 172	10 C3	
Egginton 564	10 D4	
Elmton 5,016	9 G5	
Elton 418	8 D6	
Elvaston 542	11 E4	
Etwall 2,534	10 D4	
Eyam 1,018	8 C5	
Fenny Bentley 152	10 C2	
Fernilee	8 A4	
Findern 1,784	10 D4	
Flagg 149	8 B6	
Foolow 147	8 C4	
Foremark 38	11 E5	
Foston & Scropton 496	10 C4	
Fritchley	11 E1	
Froggatt 217	8 D5	
Glapwell 1,636	9 F6	
Glossop 26,834	8 A2	
Grassmoor, Hasland &		
Winsick 3,563	9 E6	
Gratton 19	*	
Great Hucklow 141	8 C4	
Great Longstone 732	8 C5	
Green Fairfield 100	*	
Grindleford 895	*	
Grindlow 39	8 C4	
Hadfield	8 A1	
Hardstoff	9 F6	
Harpur Hill	8 B5	
Harthill 50	*	
Hartington Middle		
Quarter 355	8 C6	
Hartington Nether		
Quarter 417	8 C6	
Hartington Town		
Quarter 382	8 C6	
Hartington Upper		
Quarter 393	8 C6	
Hartshorne 3,593	11 E5	
Hasland, Grassmoor &		
Winsick 3,563	9 E5	
Hassop 72	8 C5	
Hathersage 1,352	8 D4	
Hatton 2,397	10 C4	
Hayfield 2,567	8 A3	
Hazelwood 296	11 E2	
Hazlebadge 36	*	
Heage	11 E2	
Heanor & Loscoe 15,554	11 F2	
Heath &		
Holmewood 3,032	9 F6	
High Cross Bank	10 D6	
Highlow 29	*	
Hilton 1,755	10 D4	

Place	Population	Grid
Hodthorpe		9 G4
Hognaston	243	10 D2
Holbrook	1,583	11 E2
Hollington	168	10 C3
Holmesfield	1,014	9 D4
Holmewood & Heath	3,032	9 F6
Holymoorside & Walton	1,685	9 E5
Hoon	49	*
Hope	900	8 C4
Hope Woodlands	61	*
Hopton	98	*
Hopwell	17	*
Horsley	659	11 E2
Horsley Woodhouse	1,300	11 E2
Hulland	158	10 D2
Hulland Ward	1,009	*
Hungry Bentley	58	*
Ible	39	10 D1
Idridgehay & Alton	279	10 D2
Ilkeston	33,826	11 F3
Ingleby	73	*
Ironville	1,580	11 F1
Ivonbrook Grange	23	*
Kedleston	66	10 D3
Kilburn	3,944	11 E2
Killamarsh	8,872	9 F4
King Sterndale	120	8 B5
Kirk Hallam		11 F3
Kirk Ireton	456	10 D2
Kirk Langley	577	10 D3
Kniveton	326	10 C2
Lea Hall	14	*
Lees		10 D3
Linton	2,391	10 D6
Little Eaton	2,445	11 E3
Little Hucklow	86	8 C4
Little Longstone	96	8 C5
Littleover		11 E4
Litton	548	8 C5
Long Eaton	35,251	11 F4
Longcliffe		10 C1
Longford	325	10 C3
Loscoe & Heanor	15,554	11 F2
Lullington	112	10 D6
Mackworth	159	10 D3
Mapleton	162	10 C2
Mapperley	278	11 F3
Marston Montgomery	338	10 B3
Marston on Dove	42	10 D4
Matlock Town	9,547	8 D6
Matlock Bath	918	10 D1
Melbourne	4,316	11 E5
Mercaston	65	*
Mickleover		10 D4
Middleton		10 D1
Middleton & Smerrill	158	8 C6
Milford		11 E2
Miller's Dale		8 B5
Milltown		9 E6
Monyash	283	8 C6
Moorhall		8 D5
Morley	430	11 E3
Morton	1231	9 E6
Muggington		10 D3
Nether Haddon	14	*
Nether Padley		8 D4
Netherseal	786	10 D6
New Houghton		9 F6
New Mills	9,236	8 A4
Newbold		9 E5
Newhall		11 D5
Newton Grange	47	*
Newton Solney	609	10 D5
Norbury & Roston	274	10 B3
Normanton		11 E4
North Wingfield	6,078	9 E6
Northwood & Tinkersley	659	*
Ockbrook	7,092	11 F3
Offcote & Underwood	422	*
Offerton	13	*
Old Bolsover	11,232	9 F5
Osleston & Thurvaston	257	10 D3
Osmaston	173	10 C2
Outseats	517	*
Over Haddon	225	8 C6
Overseal	2,005	10 D6
Palterton		9 F6
Parwich	516	10 C1
Peak Dale		8 B4
Peak Forest	332	8 B4
Pentrich	184	11 E1
Pikehall		10 C1
Pilsley	143	8 D5
Pilsley	3,344	9 F6
Pinxton	5,010	11 F2
Pleasley	2,278	9 F6
Quarndon	892	11 E3
Radbourne	125	*
Ravensdale Park	21	*
Renishaw		9 F4
Repton	2,306	10 D5
Ripley	19,636	11 E2
Risley	620	11 F3
Rodsley	83	10 C3
Rosliston	543	10 D6
Rowland	40	8 C5
Rowsley	451	8 D6
Sandiacre	8,525	11 F3
Scarcliffe	5,626	9 G5
Shardlow & Great Wilne	1,064	11 F4
Sheldon	97	8 C5
Shipley	735	*
Shirebrook	9,149	9 G6
Shirland & Higham	4,789	11 E1
Shirley	259	10 C3
Shottle & Postern	266	10 D2
Shuttlewood		9 F5
Slackhall		8 B3
Smalley	2,049	11 F2
Smisby	223	11 E5
Snelston	163	10 C3
Somercotes	5,728	*
Somersal Herbert	72	10 B3
South Darley	752	*
South Normanton	8,034	11 F1
South Wingfield	1,448	11 E1
Sparrowpit		8 B4
Spondon		11 E3
Stanley	2,236	11 F3
Stanton	385	*
Stanton by Bridge	212	11 E4
Stanton by Dale	473	11 F3
Stanton in Peak		8 D6
Staveley	16,544	9 F5
Stenson Fields	3,326	*
Stoke	55	*
Stonebroom		11 F1
Stoney Middleton	457	8 C5
Stretton	547	9 E6
Sudbury	643	10 C4
Sutton cum Duckmanton	1,404	9 F5
Sutton on the Hill	125	10 D4
Swadlincote	24,937	10 D5
Swanwick	4,198	*
Swarkestone	178	11 E4
Taddington	398	8 C5
Tansley	1,229	10 E1
Taxal		8 A4
Temple Normanton	432	9 F6
Thornhill	179	8 C4
Thorpe	201	10 C2
Tibshelf	3,395	9 F6
Ticknall	606	11 E5
Tideswell	1,717	8 C5
Tintwistle	1,336	8 A2
Tissington	140	10 C1
Trusley	88	10 D3
Tupton	2,934	9 E6
Turnditch	291	10 D2
Two Dales		8 D6
Twyford & Stenson	108	*
Unstone	1,907	9 E4
Upper End		8 B5
Upper Hackney		8 D6
Upper Langwith		9 G6
Wadshelf		8 D5
Walton upon Trent	924	10 C5
Walton & Holymoorside	1,685	9 E5
Wardlow	117	8 C5
Wensley		8 D6
Wessington	537	11 E1
West Hallam	5,085	11 F3
West Handley		9 E4
Westhouses		11 F2
Weston Underwood	325	10 D3
Weston upon Trent	882	11 E4
Whaley		9 G5
Whaley Bridge	5,892	8 A4
Whatstandwell		11 E1
Wheston	50	*
Whitwell	4,866	9 G5
Willington	2,292	10 D4
Windley	149	10 D2
Wingerworth	6,902	9 E6
Winster	684	8 D6
Wirksworth	5,720	10 D1
Woodthorpe		9 F5
Woodville	2,570	10 D5
Wormhill	977	8 B5
Yeaveley	262	10 C3
Yeldersley	220	*
Youlgreave	1,256	8 C6

Population figures are based upon the 1991 census and relate to the local authority area or parish as constituted at that date. Boundaries of the districts are shown on pages 4-5. Places with no population figure form part of a larger local authority area or parish.

Population figures in bold type.

*Place not included on map due to limitation of space

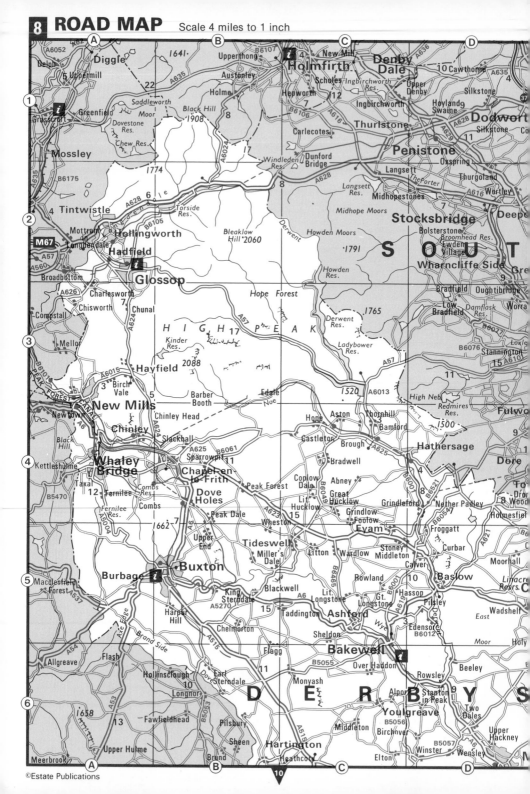

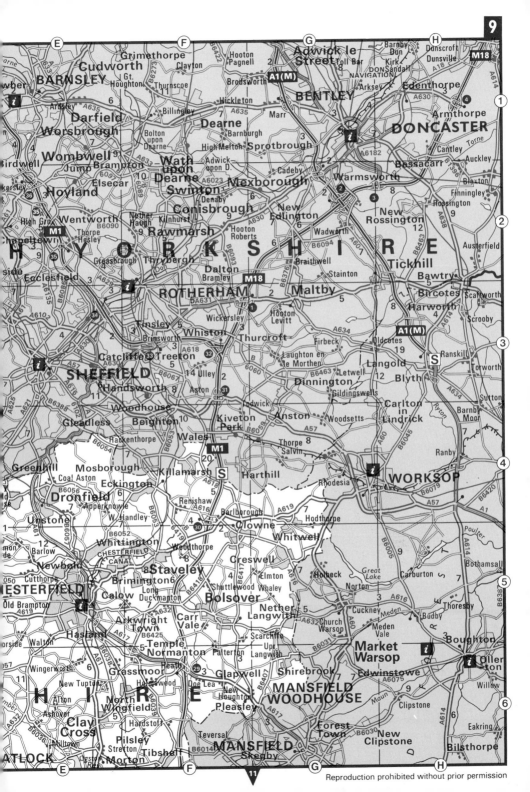

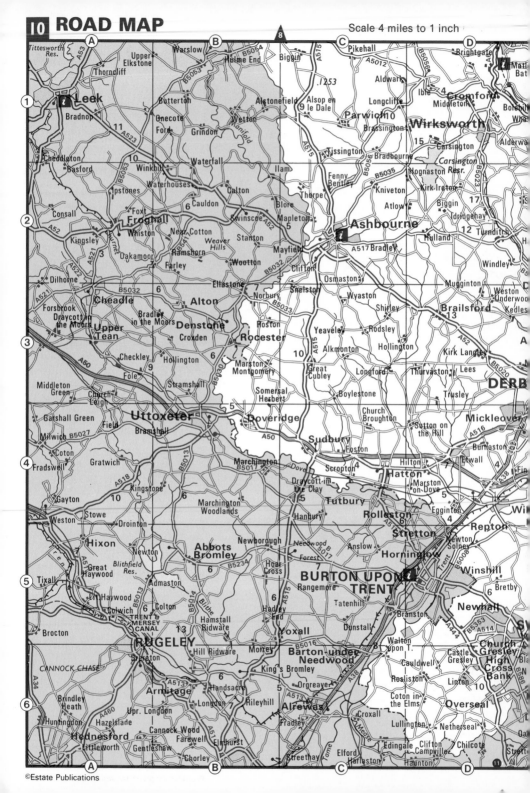

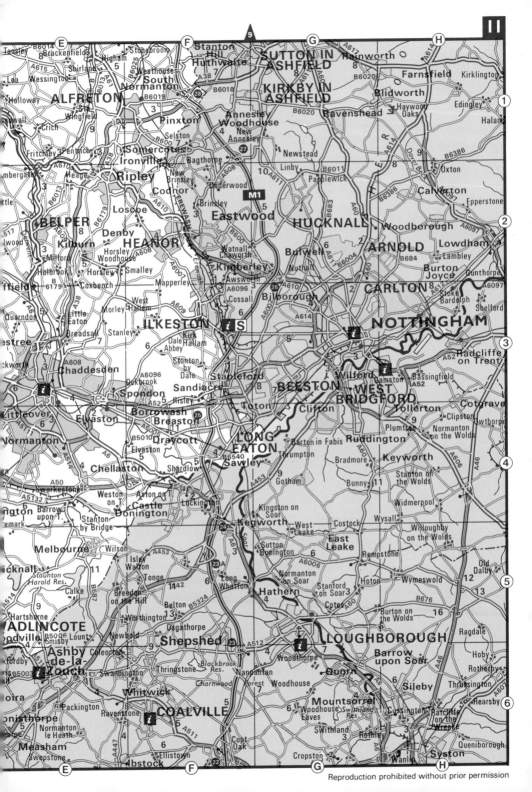

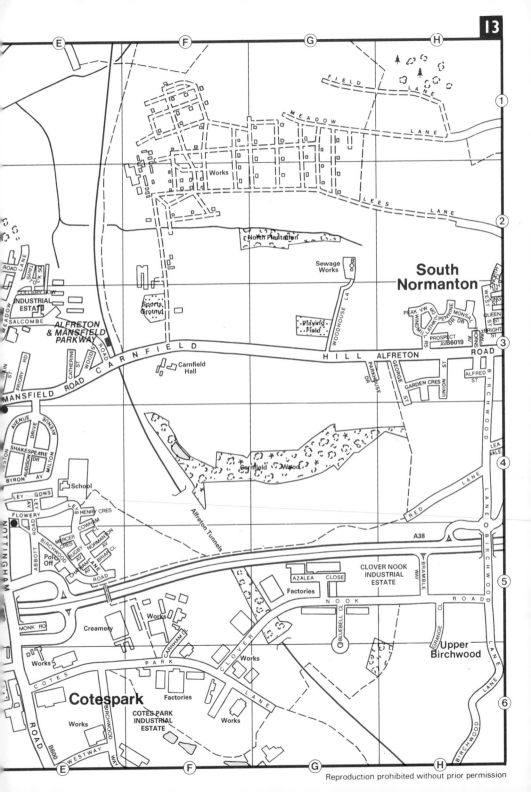

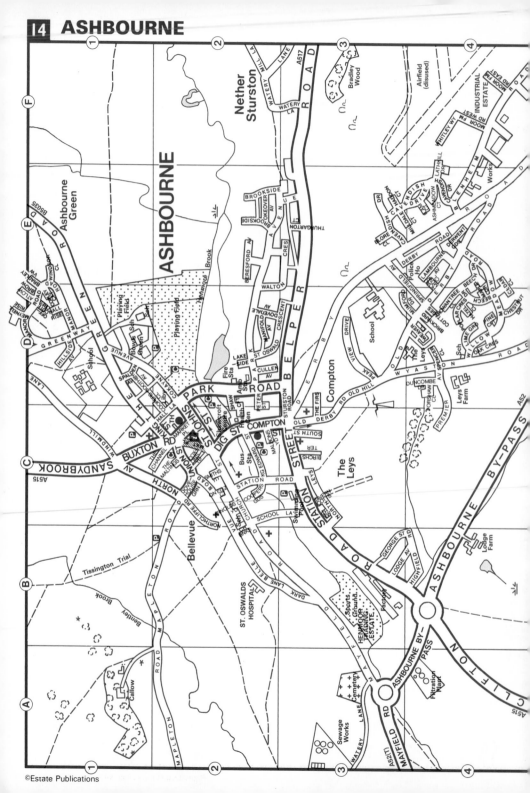

14 ASHBOURNE

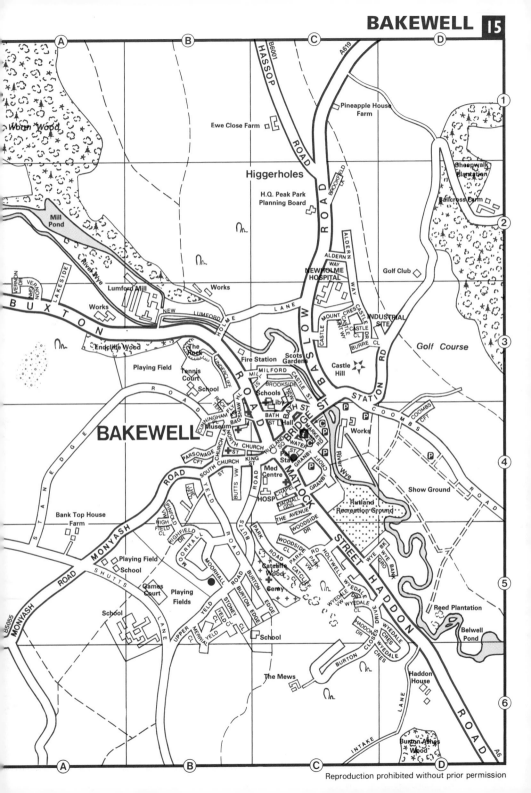

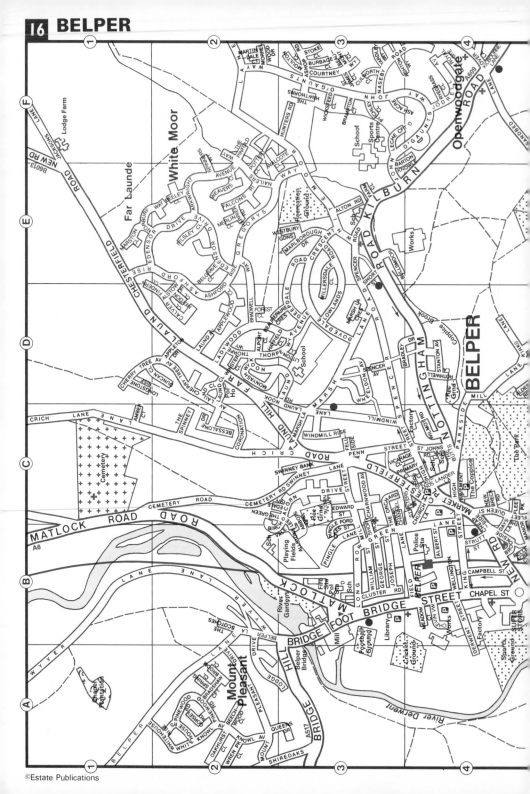

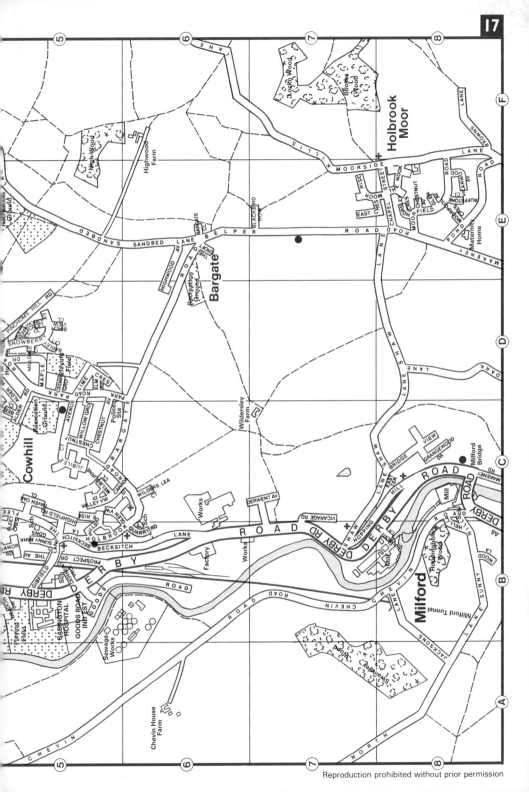

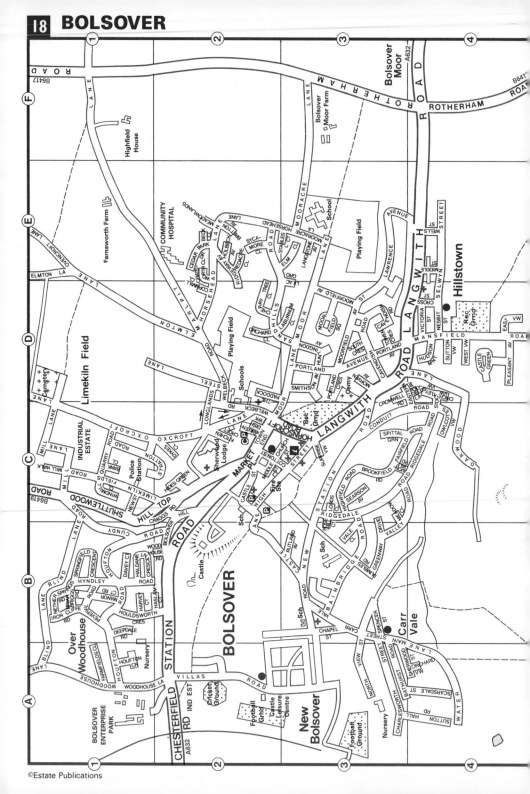

18 BOLSOVER

©Estate Publications

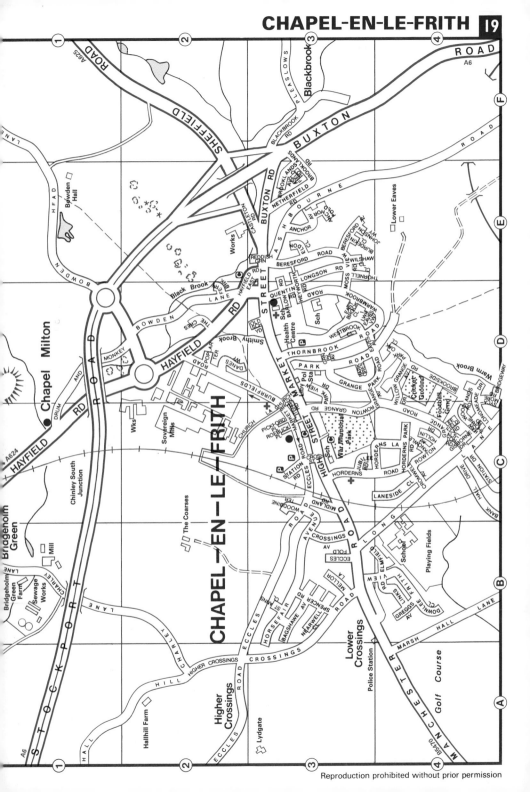

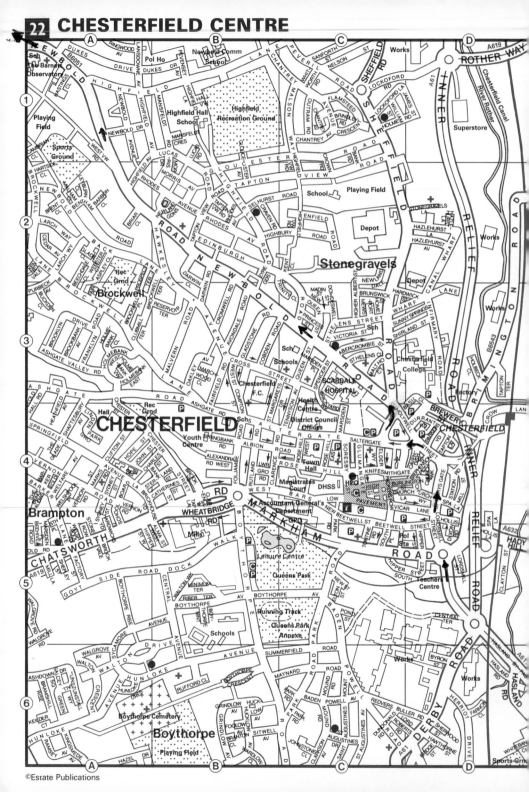

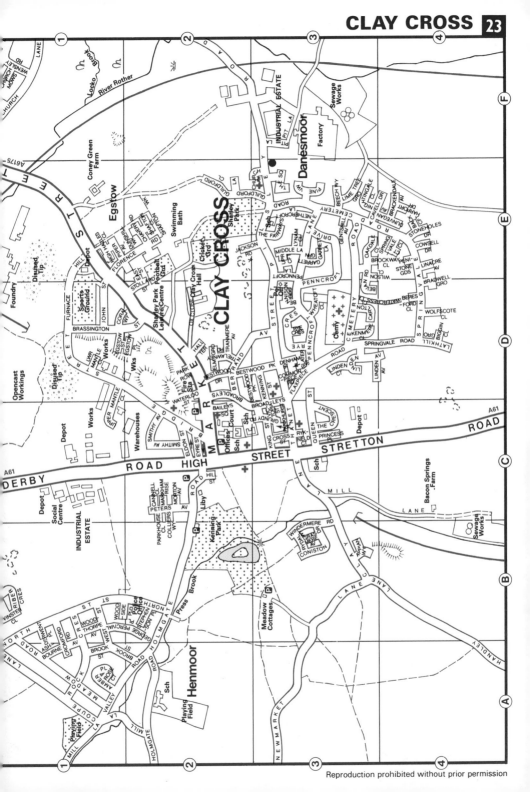

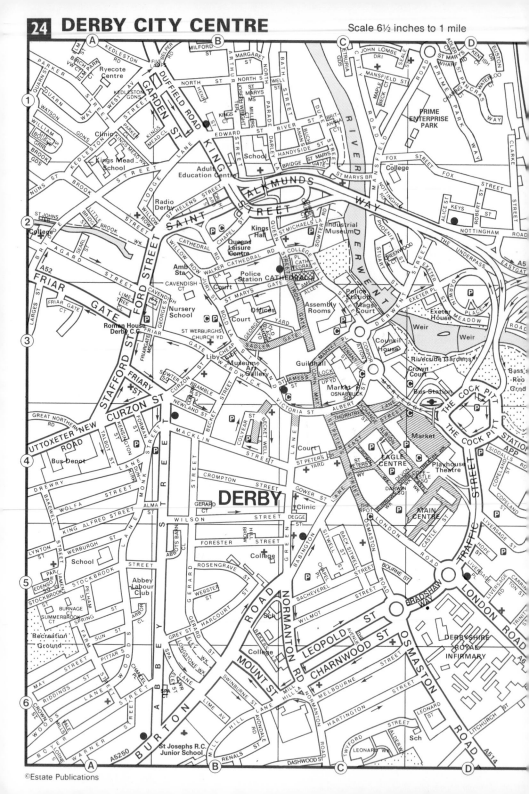

DERBY

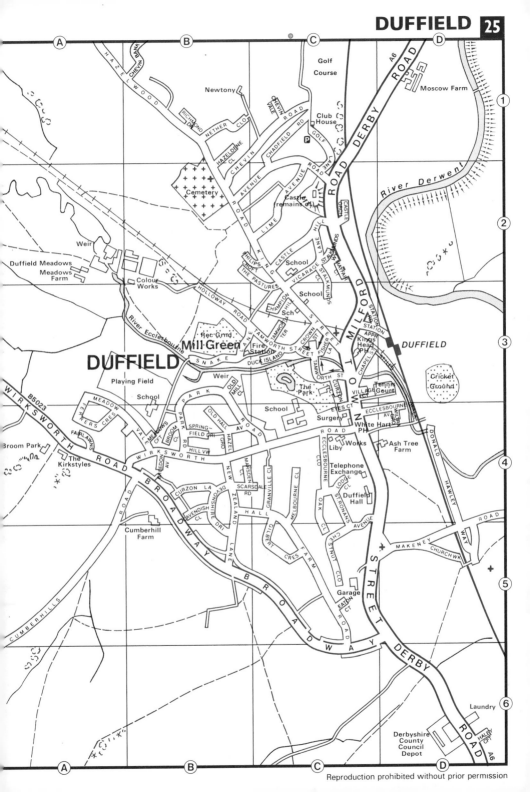

DUFFIELD

Mill Green

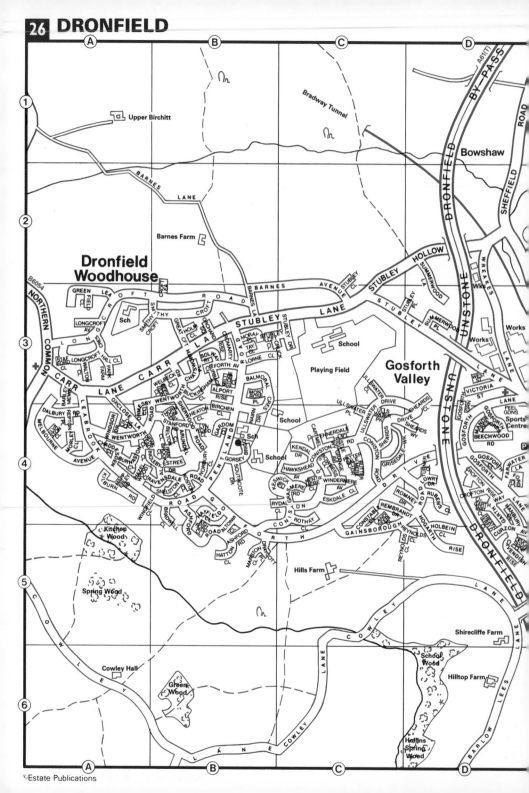

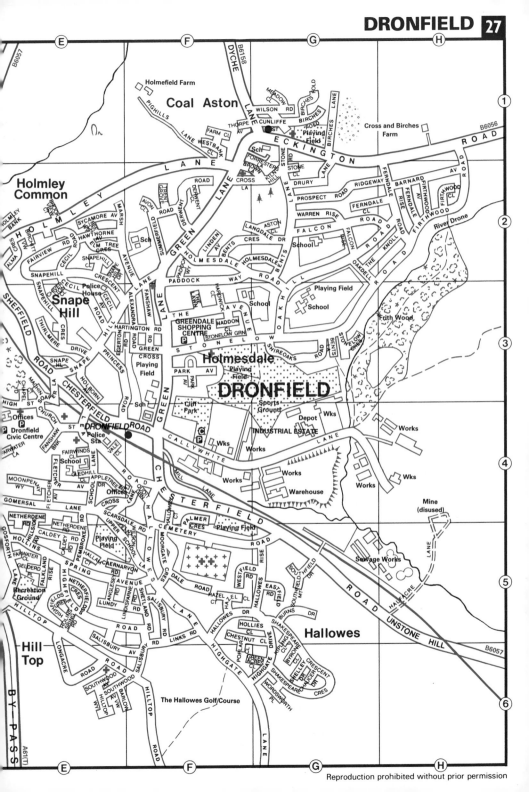

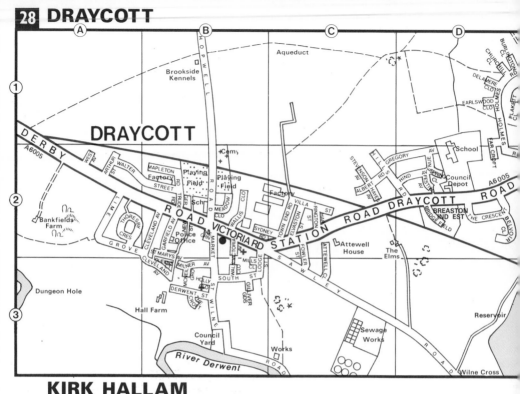

DRAYCOTT

KIRK HALLAM

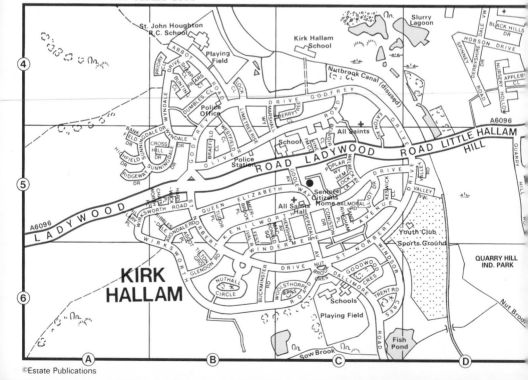

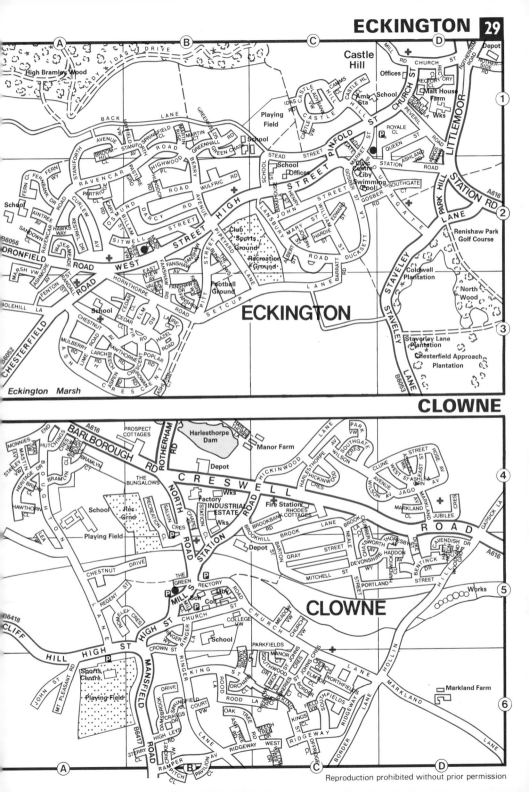

CLOWNE

ECKINGTON

CLOWNE

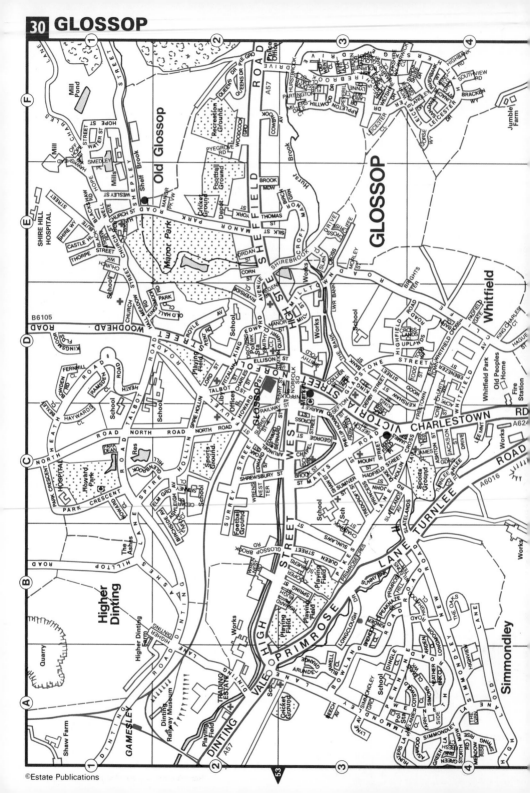

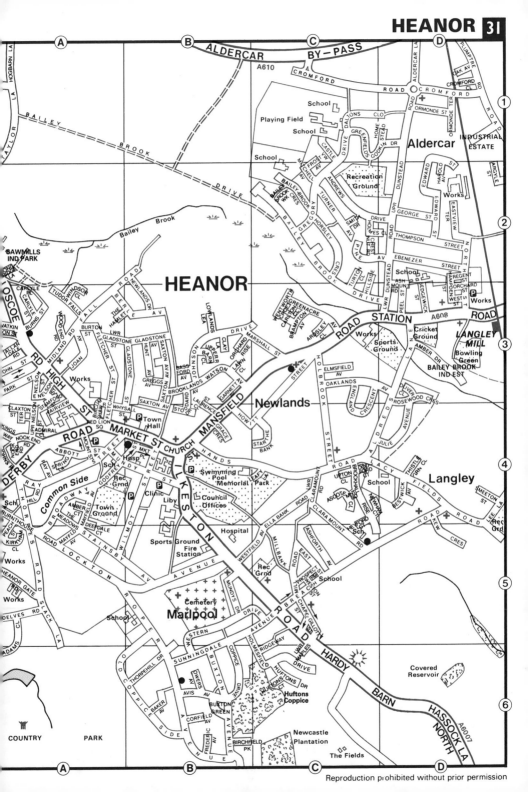

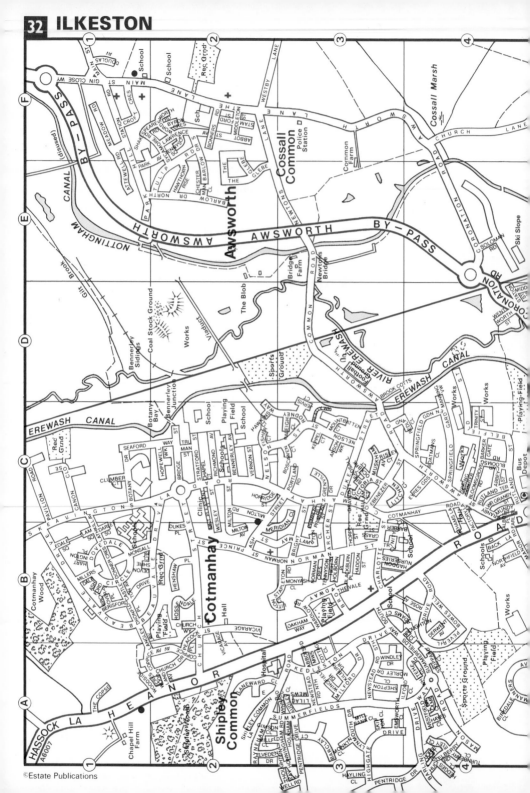

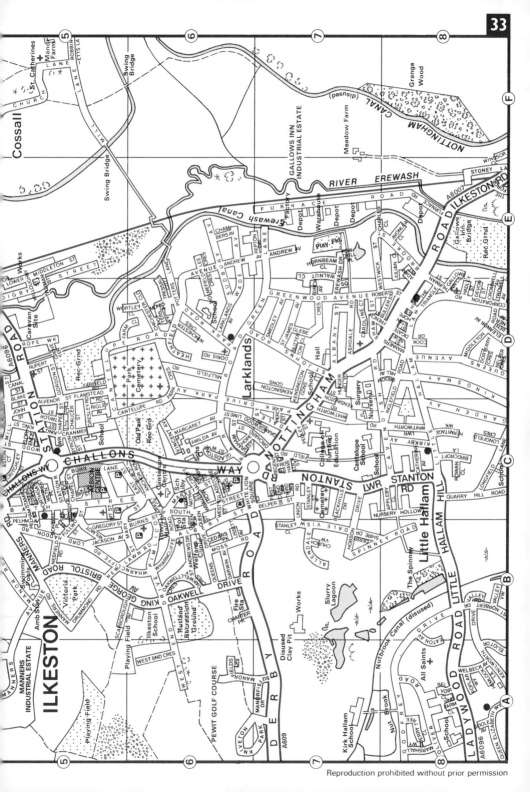

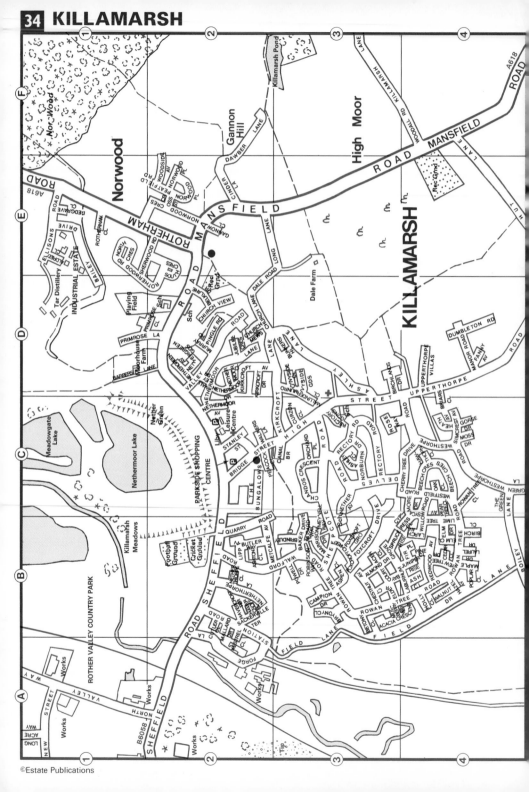

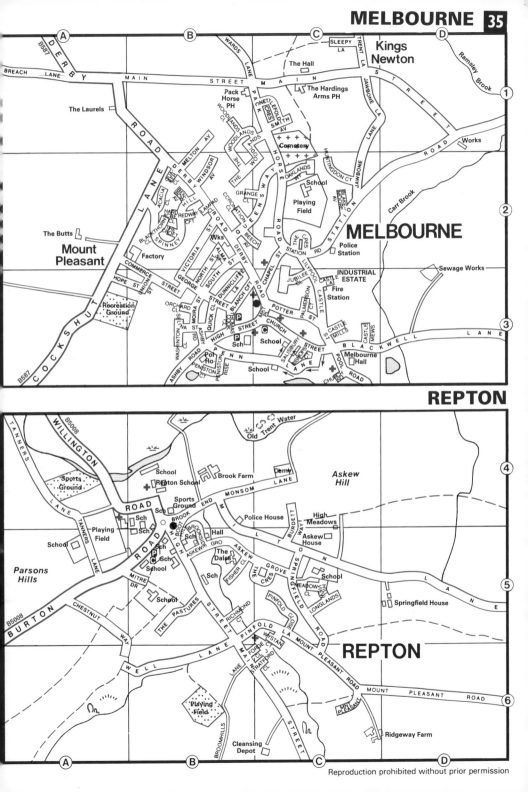

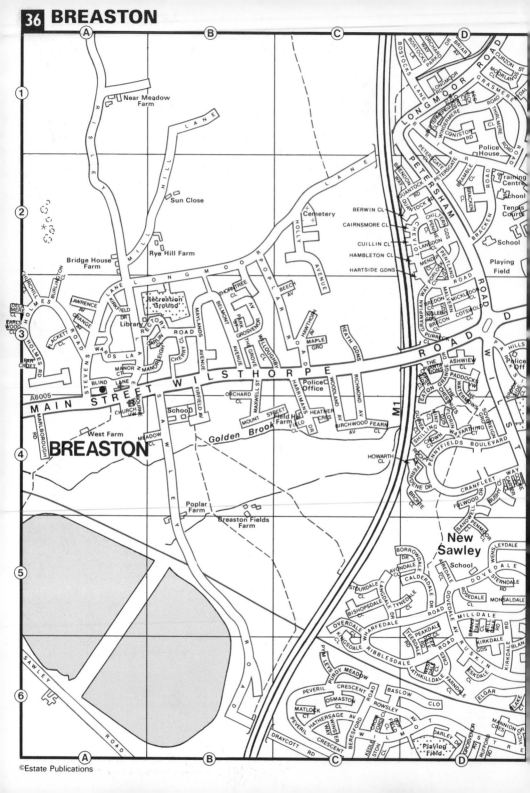

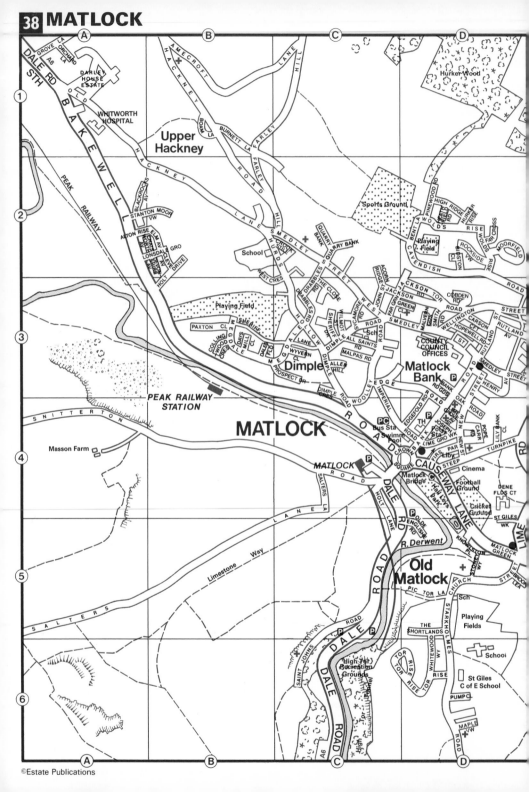

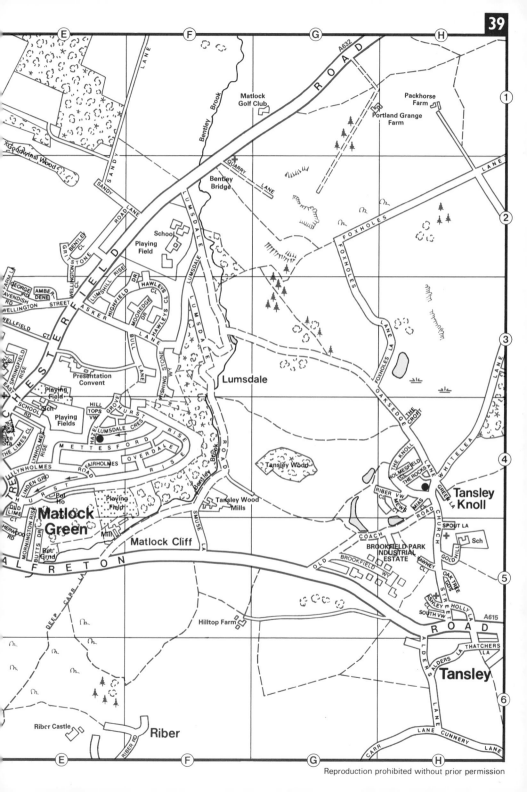

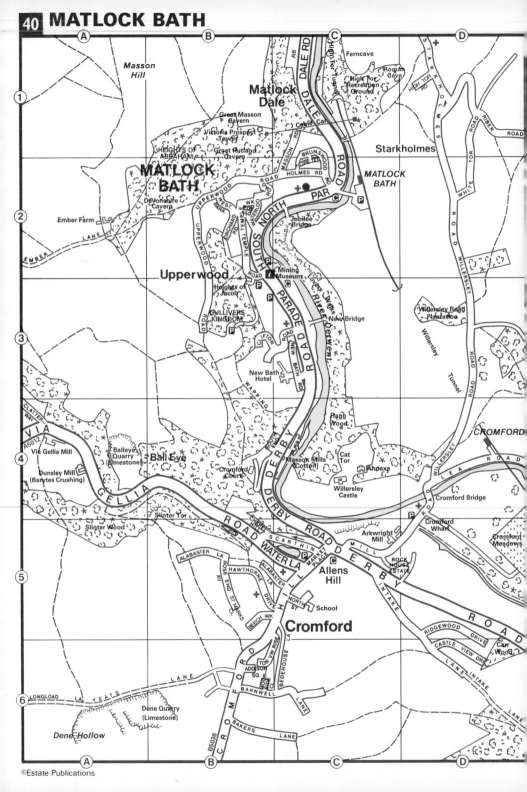

Masson Hill

Matlock Dale

Ferncave

High Tor Tunnel

Roman Cave

High Tor Recreation Ground

HIGH TOR RD

Great Masson Cavern

Victoria Prospect Tower

Cable Car

Starkholmes

HEIGHTS OF ABRAHAM

Great Rutland Cavern

MATLOCK BATH

MASSON ROAD

BRUNSWOOD ROAD

HOLMES RD

MATLOCK BATH

Devonshire Cavern

Ember Farm

EMBER LANE

UPPERWOOD WEST BANK

ORCHARD ROAD

TEMPLE ROAD

WK FOR HOTELS

NORTH PAR

Jubilee Bridge

Upperwood

Mining Museum

Heights of Jacob

GULLIVERS KINGDOM

SOUTH PARADE ROAD

Lovers Walks

River Derwent

New Bridge

WILLERSLEY ROAD

Willersley Road Plantation

Willersley

New Bath Hotel

WAPPING ROAD

NEW BATH RD

Hagg Wood

Tunnel

CROMFORD

VIA CLATTER WAY

A5012

VIA GELLIA MILL

Via Gellia Mill

Dunsley Mill (Barytes Crushing)

GELLIA ROAD

Balleye Quarry (Limestone)

Ball Eye

Cromford Court

DERBY ROAD

Masson Mills (Cotton)

Cat Tor

Annexe

LEA ROAD

Cromford Bridge

Slinter Tor

Slinter Wood

DERBY ROAD

WATER LA

SCARTHIN

Market Place

Willersley Castle

Arkwright Mill

Cromford Wharf

Cromford Meadows

ROCK HOUSE ESTATE

ALABASTER LA

ROSE END ST MARKS AV

HAWTHORNE DRIVE

ALABASTER LA

BEECH WK

NORTH ST

Allens Hill

School

MILL ROAD

DERBY ROAD

ROAD

RIDGEWOOD DRIVE

CASTLE VIEW DRIVE

LANE INTAKE

Carr Wood

Cromford

CROMFORD

TOR VW RISE

ADDISON SQ

BEDEHOUSE LA

CROMFORD ROAD

LONGLOAD LA

YEATS LANE

BARNWELL LANE

BAKERS LANE

B5036

Dene Quarry (Limestone)

Dene Hollow

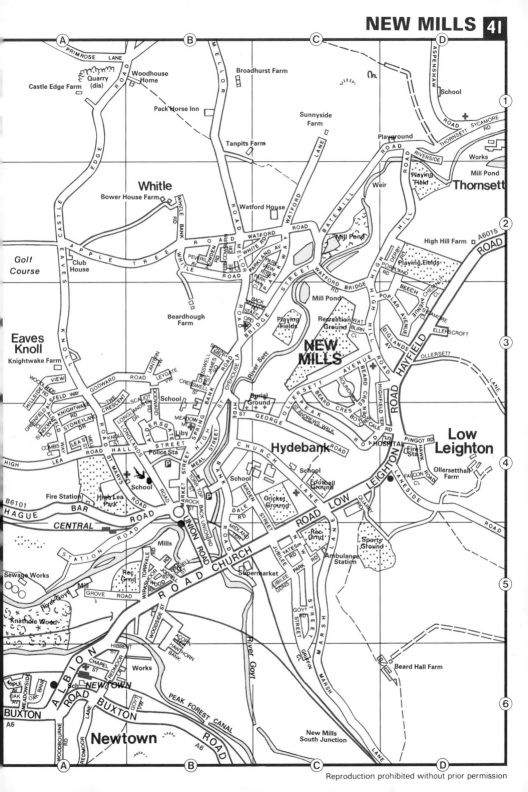

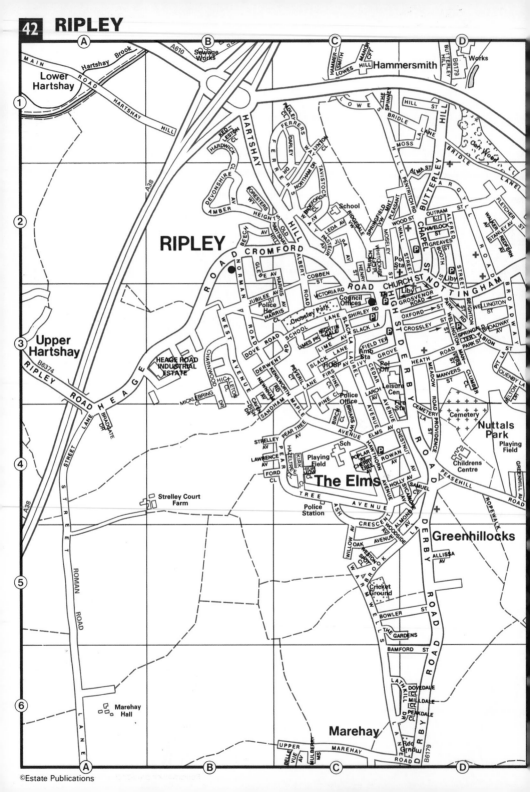

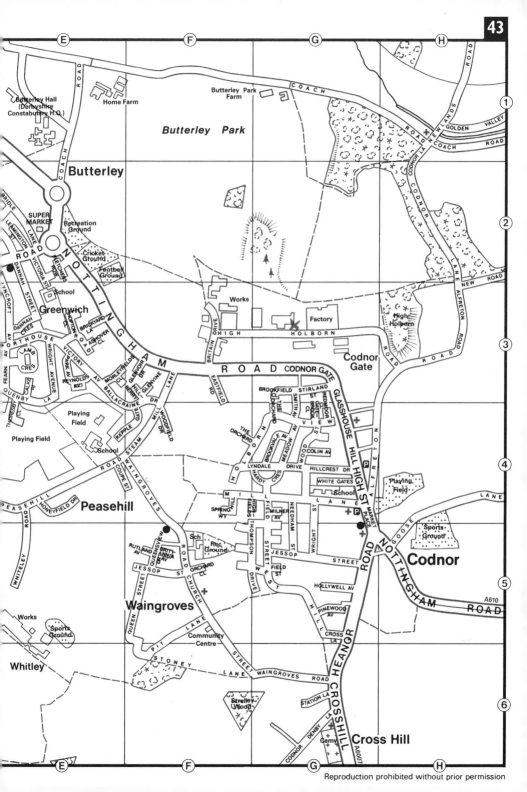

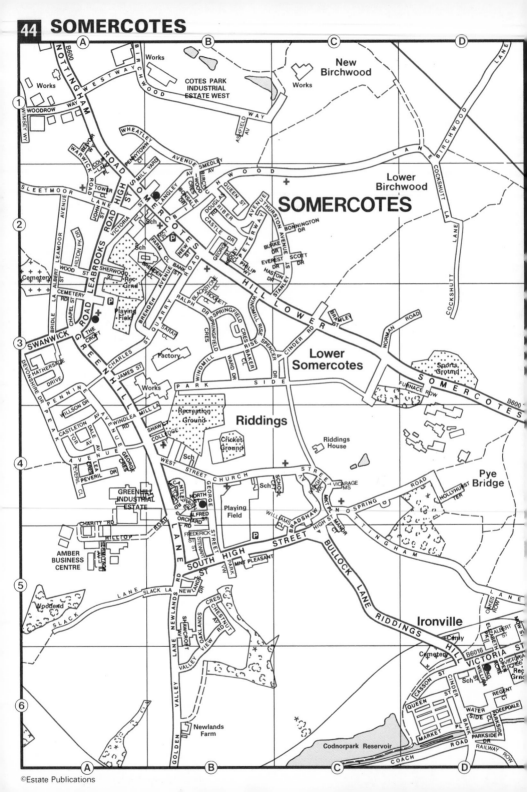

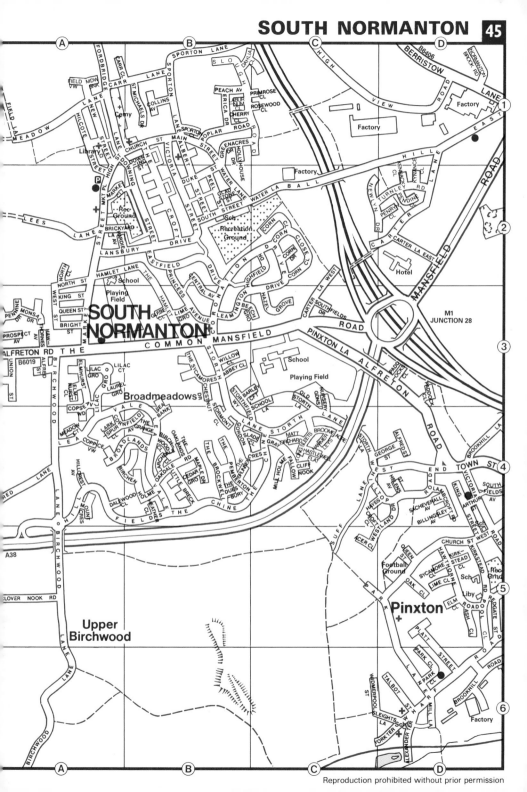

SOUTH NORMANTON

Broadmeadows

Pinxton

Upper Birchwood

M1 JUNCTION 28

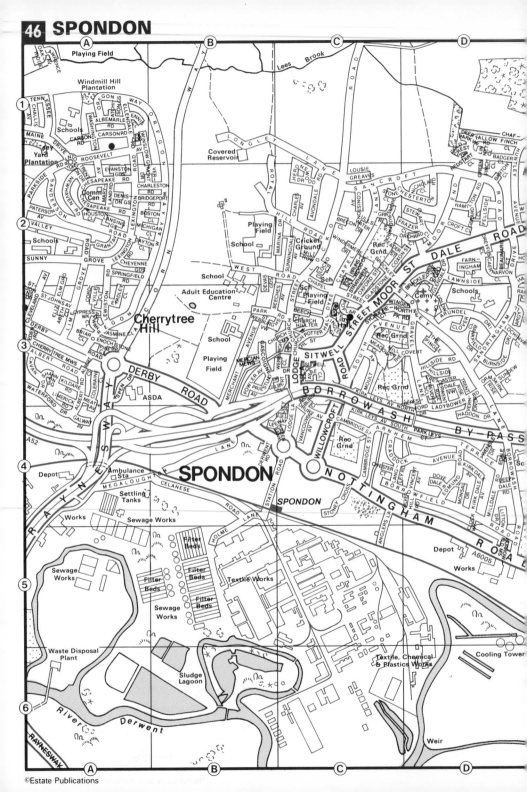

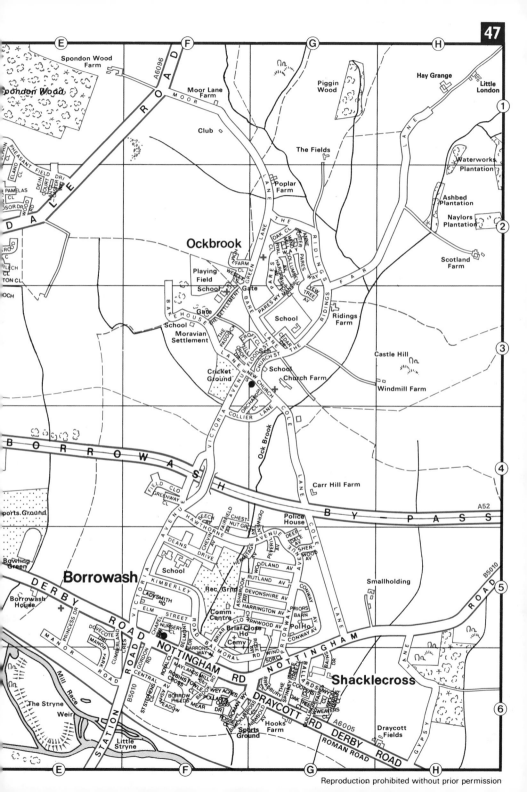

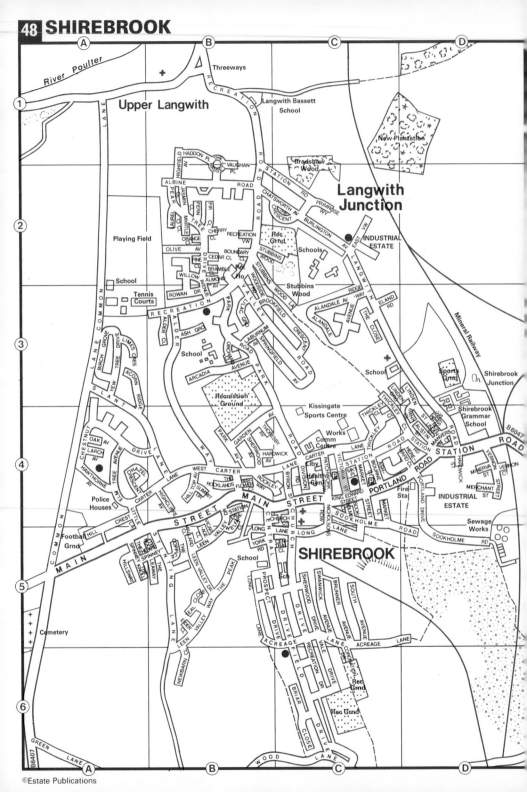

A B C D

River Poulter

Threeways

Upper Langwith

Langwith Bassett
School

New Plantation

Bradshaw
Wood

Langwith
Junction

INDUSTRIAL
ESTATE

Playing Field

Rec.
Grnd

Schools

Mineral Railway

School

Recreation
Grnd

Stubbins
Wood

Stubbins
Wood

Shirebrook
Junction

Tennis
Courts

Sports
Grnd

School

Shirebrook
Grammar
School

B6047

School

Kissingate
Sports Centre

Recreation
Ground

Works
Comm
Centre

Police
Houses

WEST
CARTER

Liby
Health
Cent.

PORTLAND ROAD

STATION ROAD

INDUSTRIAL
ESTATE

Fire
Sta.

Football
Grnd

MAIN STREET

CHURCH

Sewage
Works

School

SHIREBROOK

Cemetery

Sch

Rec
Grnd

WOOD LANE

Rec Grnd

B6407 GREEN LANE

©Estate Publications

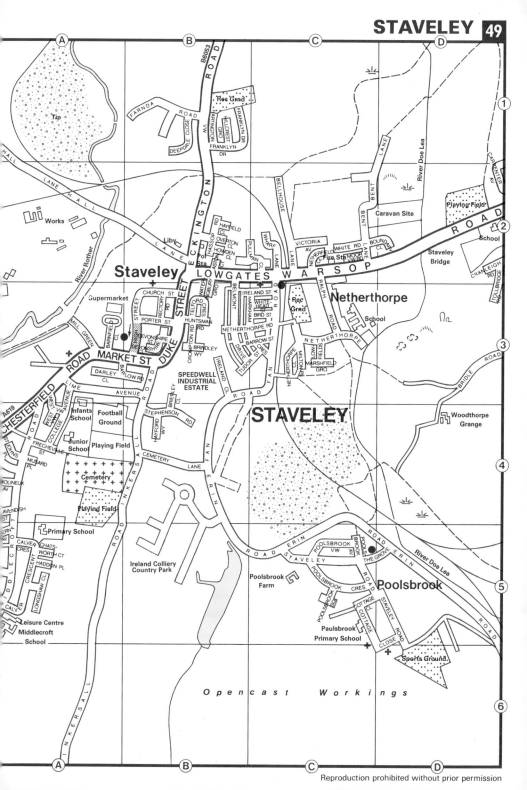

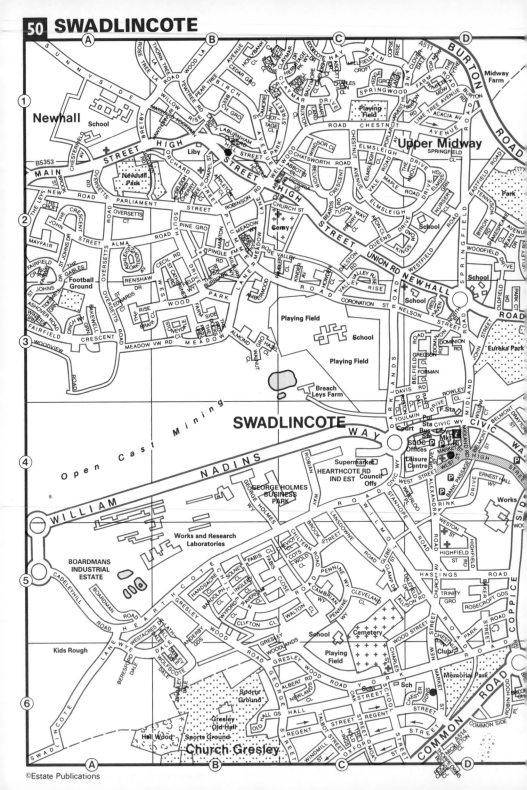

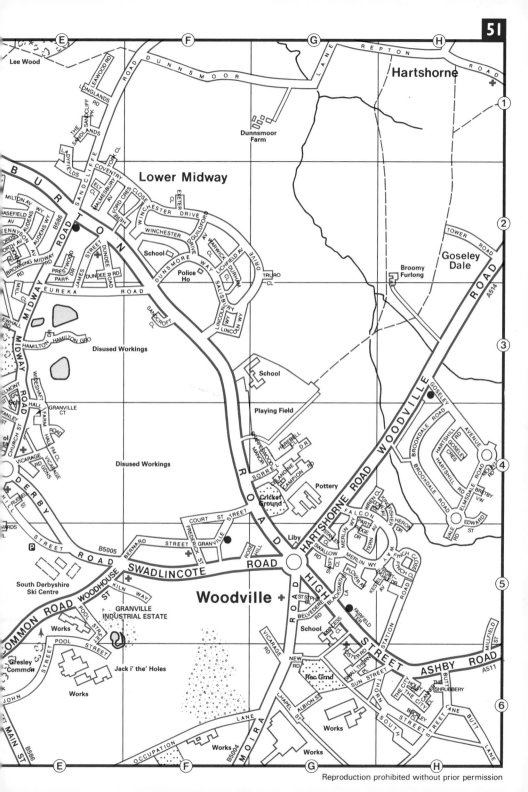

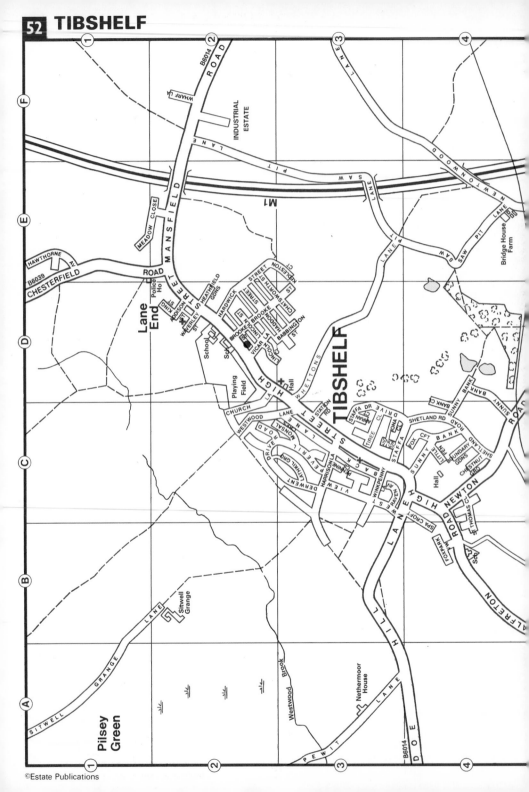

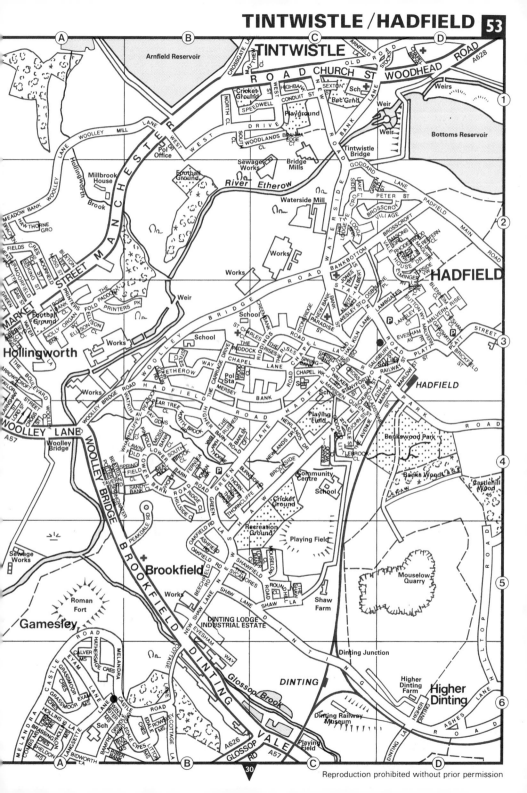

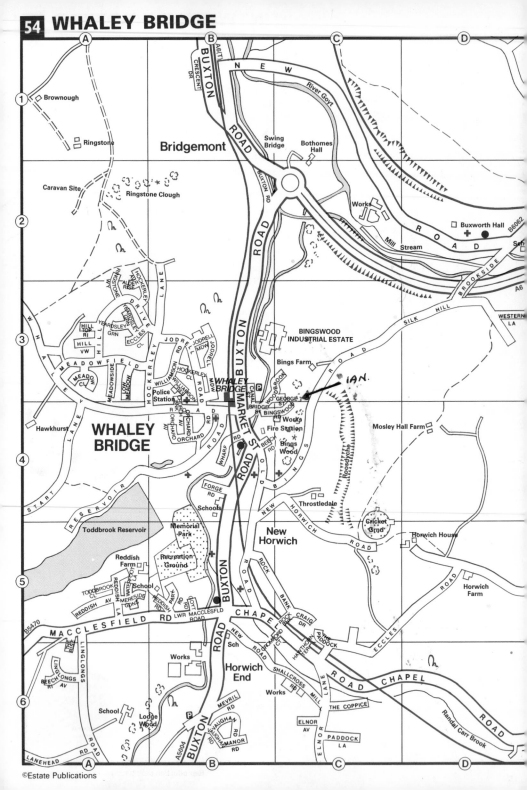

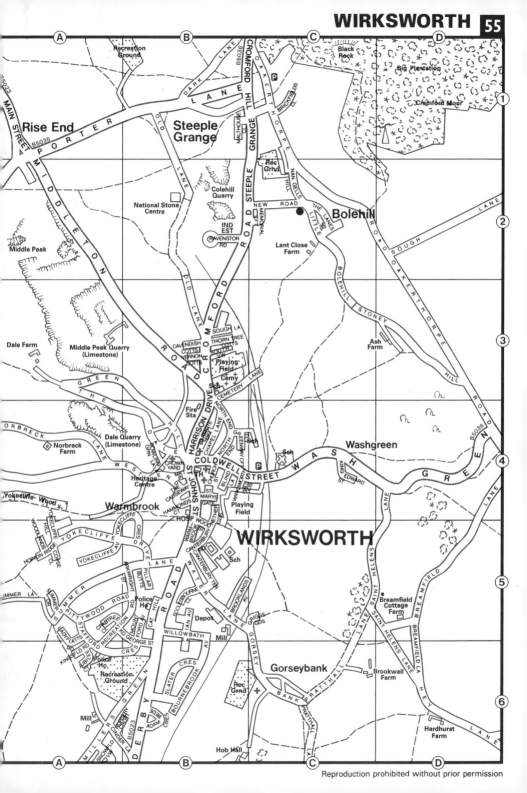

The Index includes some names for which there is insufficient space on the maps. These names are preceded by an * and are followed by the nearest adjoining thoroughfare.

ALFRETON

Abbott Rd. DE55	13 E5
Addison Dri. DE55	13 E4
Alfred St, Alfreton. DE55	12 C5
Alfred St, South Normanton. DE55	13 H3
Alfreton By-Pass. DE55	12 B6
Alfreton Rd. DE55	13 H3
Alma St. DE55	12 D4
Amber Gro. DE55	12 C3
Arthur St. DE55	12 C3
Azalea Clo. DE55	13 G5
Beech Av. DE55	12 D3
Bentley Clo. DE55	12 D3
Birch Clo. DE55	12 D3
Birchwood La. DE55	13 H3
Birchwood Rd. DE55	13 E5
Birchwood Way. DE55	13 E6
Bishop St. DE55	13 G5
Bluebell Clo. DE55	13 G5
Bonsall La. DE55	12 C4
Bramble Way. DE55	13 H5
Briar Clo. DE55	13 E5
Bright St. DE55	13 H3
Brook Av. DE55	12 D5
Brook Clo. DE55	12 D5
Brook La. DE55	12 D5
Byron Av. DE55	13 E4
Carnfield Hill. DE55	13 E3
Carnham Clo. DE55	13 F6
Catherine St. DE55	13 E3
Cedar Av. DE55	12 C3
Central Rd. DE55	12 C4
Chapel St. DE55	12 C4
Charles St. DE55	12 C3
Chatham Av. DE55	13 E5
Chatsworth Clo. DE55	12 C4
Chesterfield Rd. DE55	12 B1
Church St. DE55	12 C4
Clover Nook Rd. DE55	13 F6
Colin St. DE55	12 D4
Colliery Rd. DE55	12 B5
Colliery Row. DE55	13 E3
Connaught Ct. DE55	12 D4
Cornhill Dri. DE55	12 D4
Cotes Park La. DE55	13 E6
Cowham Clo. DE55	13 E4
Cressy Rd. DE55	12 C4
Derby Rd. DE55	12 B5
Derwent Gro. DE55	12 C5
Dunsford Rd. DE55	12 D2
Eachwell La. DE55	12 B5
Ellesmere Av. DE55	12 D4
Elms Av. DE55	12 D3
Elms Clo. DE55	12 D3
Ewart La. DE55	12 B5
Field La. DE55	13 G1
Firs Av. DE55	12 D3
Firs Gdns. DE55	12 D3
Flowery Leys La. DE55	13 E4
Frederick St. DE55	12 C3
Garden Cres. DE55	13 H3
George St, Alfreton. DE55	12 D4
George St, South Normanton. DE55	13 H3
Gladstone Rd. DE55	12 C5
Gooker La. DE55	12 B5
Grange Clo. DE55	13 H5
Grange St. DE55	12 C4
Haddon Clo. DE55	12 B5
Hall St. DE55	12 C4
Hardy St. DE55	12 C3
Hawthorns Av. DE55	13 H3
Henry Cres. DE55	13 E4
High St. DE55	12 C4
Hockley Way. DE55	12 D6

Independent Hill. DE55	12 C5
INDUSTRIAL ESTATES:	
Clover Nook Ind Est. DE55	13 G5
Cotes Park Ind Est. DE55	13 F6
Nixs Hill Ind Est. DE55	13 F6
Institute La. DE55	12 C4
John St. DE55	12 D4
Keys Rd. DE55	12 D5
King St. DE55	12 C5
King St, South Normanton. DE55	13 H3
Lathkill Dri. DE55	13 H3
Lea Vale. DE55	13 H4
Lees La. DE55	13 G2
Ley Av. DE55	13 E4
Ley Gdns. DE55	13 E4
Limes Av. DE55	12 C4
Lincoln St. DE55	12 C4
Long Meadow Rd. DE55	12 B5
Lydford Rd. DE55	12 D4
Mansfield Rd. DE55	12 D4
Marshall St. DE55	12 C4
Meadow La, Alfreton. DE55	12 D3
Meadow La, South Normanton. DE55	13 G1
Mercer Cres. DE55	13 E5
Milton Av. DE55	13 E4
Monk St. DE55	13 E5
Monsal St. DE55	13 H3
New St. DE55	12 C4
Nixs Hill. DE55	13 E5
Normanton Av. DE55	13 E5
North Clo. DE55	13 H3
North St. DE55	12 D5
North St, South Normanton. DE55	13 H3
Nottingham Rd. DE55	12 D4
Nuttall Clo. DE55	12 C5
Nuttall St. DE55	12 C5
Oak Dri. DE55	12 D3
Oakland St. DE55	12 D4
Orange St. DE55	12 D4
Outseats Dri. DE55	12 D5
Park St. DE55	12 C5
Parkhouse Dri. DE55	13 G3
Parkin St. DE55	13 E3
Peak View. DE55	13 H3
Pease Clo. DE55	12 D5
Pease Hill. DE55	12 D5
Pennine Dri. DE55	13 H3
Preston Av. DE55	13 E4
Priory St. DE55	13 E3
Prospect Av. DE55	13 H3
Prospect St. DE55	12 D4
Providence Pl. DE55	12 C5
Queen St. DE55	13 H3
Raglan St. DE55	12 D4
Red La. DE55	13 H4
Roberts Dri. DE55	12 C4
Rodgers La. DE55	12 C4
Rowland St. DE55	12 C3
Rugby Av. DE55	13 E5
Salcombe Rd. DE55	13 E3
Severn Sq. DE55	12 C4
Shakespeare Dri. DE55	13 E4
South Croft. DE55	12 D5
Tavistock Sq. DE55	13 E2
The Crescent. DE55	12 D5
The Green. DE55	12 D5
Trent Gro. DE55	12 C5
Union St. DE55	13 H3
Venture Cres. DE55	13 D6
Victoria St. DE55	12 D4
West End. DE55	12 D5
West End Clo. DE55	12 D5
West St. DE55	13 H3
Westway. DE55	13 E6
Whites La. DE55	12 D6
Willow Clo. DE55	12 D3
Willows Av. DE55	12 D3
Wilson St. DE55	12 D4
Wimsey Way. DE55	12 D6
Windmill Rise. DE55	13 H3

Wingfield Rd. DE55	12 A4
Wood St. DE55	13 E3
Woodhouse La. DE55	13 G3
Wycliffe Rd. DE55	12 D4

ASHBOURNE

*Arnolds Yard, Church St. DE6	14 C2
Ashbourne By-Pass. DE6	14 B4
Ashmeadow Clo. DE6	14 E4
Atlow Brow. DE6	14 D1
Arnolds Yd. DE6	14 C2
Beech Dri. DE6	14 D4
Belle Vue Rd. DE6	14 B2
Belper Rd. DE6	14 D3
Beresford Av. DE6	14 E2
Birchs Ter. DE6	14 C3
Blenheim Rd. DE6	14 E4
Blore Clo. DE6	14 E3
Boothby Av. DE6	14 D1
*Boswell Ct, Union St. DE6	14 C2
Bradley View. DE6	14 E1
Brickyard Cotts. DE6	14 D4
Brookside. DE6	14 E2
Buxton Rd. DE6	14 C1
Cavendish Dri. DE6	14 E4
Cedar Clo. DE6	14 D4
Chestnut Dri. DE6	14 D4
Church Banks. DE6	14 B2
Church St. DE6	14 C2
Church View. DE6	14 C3
Clifton Rd. DE6	14 A4
Cokayne Av. DE6	14 D2
Compton St. DE6	14 C2
Coopers Clo. DE6	14 C2
Coopers Gdns. DE6	14 D1
Copley Croft. DE6	14 D1
Coxons Yd. DE6	14 C2
Cullen St. DE6	14 D2
Dark La. DE6	14 B3
Derby Rd. DE6	14 D2
Derwent Gdns. DE6	14 E4
Dig St. DE6	14 C2
Dovedale Av. DE6	14 D2
Dovehouse Grn. DE6	14 C2
Duncombe Dri. DE6	14 D4
Forshaw Clo. DE6	14 C4
George St. DE6	14 B3
Greenway. DE6	14 D1
Haddon Ct. DE6	14 E3
Hall La. DE6	14 C2
Hall Rise. DE6	14 D1
*Hawthorn Clo, Beech Dri. DE6	14 E4
Hazel Clo. DE6	14 D4
*Henmore Pl, Shaw Croft. DE6	14 D2
Highfield Rd. DE6	14 B4
Hillside Av. DE6	14 D1
*Holly Clo, Beech Dri. DE6	14 E4
*Hoods Yard, Dig St. DE6	14 C2
*Horse & Jockey Yard, St Johns St. DE6	14 C2
Ilam Ct. DE6	14 E4
INDUSTRIAL ESTATES:	
Henmore Trading Est. DE6	14 B3
King Edward St. DE6	14 C2
King St. DE6	14 C2
Lakeside. DE6	14 D2
*Lacemakers Cotts, Buxton Rd. DE6	14 C1
Lambourne Av. DE6	14 E4
Lathkill Dri. DE6	14 E4
Lime Gro. DE6	14 D4
Lodge Av. DE6	14 B3
*Lovatts Yard, Market Pl. DE6	14 C2
Malbons Yard. DE6	14 C2
*Malthouse Ct, Hall La. DE6	14 C2

Manifold Av. DE6	14 D2
Manor Rd. DE6	14 D1
Maple Dri. DE6	14 D4
Mapleton Rd. DE6	14 A2
Market Pl. DE6	14 C2
Mayfield Rd. DE6	14 A3
Meynell Rise. DE6	14 D1
Mill La. DE6	14 F2
Milldale Ct. DE6	14 C2
Moor Farm Rd E. DE6	14 F4
Moor Farm Rd W. DE6	14 F4
Mumford Dri. DE6	14 D4
North Av. DE6	14 C2
North Leys. DE6	14 C3
Northcliffe Rd. DE6	14 C2
Oak Cres. DE6	14 D4
Offcote Cres. DE6	14 D1
Okeover Av. DE6	14 E2
Old Derby Rd. DE6	14 C3
Old Hill. DE6	14 D3
Park Av. DE6	14 D2
Park Rd. DE6	14 D2
Peak View Dri. DE6	14 D3
Peter St. DE6	14 D2
Pine Croft. DE6	14 D4
Poplar Cres. DE6	14 D4
Premier Av. DE6	14 C4
Queen Elizabeth Ct. DE6	14 C2
Roadmeadow Clo. DE6	14 E4
Rowan Tree Clo. DE6	14 D4
St Johns St. DE6	14 C2
*Salt Alley, St Johns St. DE6	14 C2
Sandybrook. DE6	14 C1
School La. DE6	14 C2
*Shakespeare Ct, Union St. DE6	14 C2
Shaw Croft. DE6	14 D2
Smiths Yard. DE6	14 B2
South St. DE6	14 C3
Spalden Av. DE6	14 D1
Spencer Clo. DE6	14 D4
Springfield Av. DE6	14 D4
Station Rd. DE6	14 C2
Station St. DE6	14 C3
Sturston Rd. DE6	14 C3
Tavern Cotts. DE6	14 C3
The Channel. DE6	14 C1
The Firs. DE6	14 C3
The Green Rd. DE6	14 C1
The Maltings. DE6	14 C2
Thurgarton Ct. DE6	14 E3
*Town Hall Yard, Hall La. DE6	14 C2
*Town Head, The Green Rd. DE6	14 C1
*Tunnel Yard, Church St. DE6	14 C2
Union St. DE6	14 C2
Walton Cres. DE6	14 E2
Watery La. DE6	14 A3
Watery La. DE6	14 F2
Weaver Clo. DE6	14 D4
Whitley Way. DE6	14 F4
Willow Meadow Rd. DE6	14 D4
Windmill La. DE6	14 C1
Windsor Clo. DE6	14 E1
Wyaston Av. DE6	14 D3

BAKEWELL

Aldern Way. DE45	15 C2
*Arkwright Sq, Mill St. DE45	15 C3
Bagshaw Hill. DE45	15 B4
Baslow Rd. DE45	15 C3
Bath St. DE45	15 C4
Bridge St. DE45	15 C4
Brookfield La. DE45	15 C3
Brookside. DE45	15 C3
Burre Clo. DE45	15 C3
Burton Closes Dri. DE45	15 C6
Burton Edge. DE45	15 B5

Butts Rd. DE45	15 B5
Butts View. DE45	15 B4
Buxton Rd. DE45	15 A3
Castle Clo. DE45	15 C3
Castle Dri. DE45	15 C3
Castle Mount Cres. DE45	15 C3
Castle Mount Way. DE45	15 C5
Catcliff Clo. DE45	15 C5
*Catcliff Cotts, Yeld Rd. DE45	15 B4
Chapel La. DE45	15 C4
Church La. DE45	15 C4
Coombs Croft. DE45	15 D4
Coombs Rd. DE45	15 D4
Cunningham Pl. DE45	15 B4
Dagnall Gdns. DE45	15 C4
Fly Hill. DE45	15 B4
Granby Croft. DE45	15 C4
Granby Rd. DE45	15 C4
Haddon Dri. DE45	15 C5
Haddon Rd. DE45	15 C4
Hassop Rd. DE45	15 C1
Highfield Clo. DE45	15 B4
Highfield Dri. DE45	15 B5
Holme La. DE45	15 B3
Holywell. DE45	15 C5
Intake La. DE45	15 C6
King St. DE45	15 B4
Lakeside. DE45	15 A3
Market St. DE45	15 C4
Matlock St. DE45	15 C4
Merrial Clo. DE45	15 B5
Milford Castle St. DE45	15 C3
Mill St. DE45	15 C3
Monyash Rd. DE45	15 A5
Moorhall. DE45	15 B5
New Lumford. DE45	15 B3
New St. DE45	15 C3
North Church St. DE45	15 C4
Park Rd. DE45	15 C5
Park View. DE45	15 C5
Parsonage Croft. DE45	15 B4
*Parsonage Ter, Cunningham Pl. DE45	15 B4
Pinfold View. DE45	15 B4
*Portland Sq, Market Sq. DE45	15 C4
Rock Ter. DE45	15 B3
Rutland Sq. DE45	15 C4
Shutts La. DE45	15 A5
South Church St. DE45	15 B4
Stanedge Rd. DE45	15 A5
Station Rd. DE45	15 C3
Stoney Clo. DE45	15 B5
The Avenue. DE45	15 C4
The Yeld. DE45	15 B4
Undercliff. DE45	15 B3
Upper Yeld Rd. DE45	15 B5
Vernon Dri. DE45	15 A3
Vernon Grn. DE45	15 A2
*Water La, Water St. DE45	15 C4
Water St. DE45	15 C4
Woodside Clo. DE45	15 C5
Woodside Dri. DE45	15 C5
Wye Bank. DE45	15 D5
Wye Bank Gro. DE45	15 D5
Wyedale Clo. DE45	15 D5
Wyedale Cres. DE45	15 D5
Wyedale Dri. DE45	15 D5
Wyedale Vw. DE45	15 C5
Yeld Clo. DE45	15 B5
Yeld Rd. DE45	15 B4

BELPER

Abbots Cro. DE56	16 C3
Acorn Dri. DE56	16 C3
Acorn Way. DE56	16 C3
Albert St. DE56	16 B4
Alder Rd. DE56	17 C5
Allstone Lee. DE56	16 B3
Alport Clo. DE56	16 D2
Alston Dri. DE56	16 D2

Alton Rd. DE56 16 E3
Amber Ct. DE56 16 C1
Appleton Dri. DE56 16 D2
Applewood Clo. DE56 16 D2
Arkwright Av. DE56 16 E2
Ash Acre. DE56 16 F3
Ashford Rise. DE56 16 D2
Ashop Rd. DE56 16 F3
Ashton Way. DE56 16 F3
Bargate Clo. DE56 17 E6
Bargate Rd. DE56 17 C5
Barley Croft. DE56 17 D5
Barton Knowle. DE56 16 E3
Beaumont Clo. DE56 16 F3
Beaurepaire Cres. DE56 16 D3
Becksitch La. DE56 17 B5
Beech Clo. DE56 17 C5
Beechwood Clo. DE56 16 A2
Beeley Clo. DE56 16 E2
Belgrave Clo. DE56 16 E2
Belle Acre Clo. DE56 16 B4
Belper La. DE56 16 A1
Belper Rd. DE56 17 E6
Bessalone Dri. DE56 16 C2
Birch Vale. DE56 16 B3
Birch View Clo. DE56 17 D5
Blackbird Row. DE56 17 E7
*Bosley Mews, Abbots Gro. DE56 16 C3
*Bradfield Clo, Naseby Rd. DE56 16 F3
Bradley Dri. DE56 16 D4
Bradshaw Croft. DE56 16 A2
Bradwell Way. DE56 16 D2
Brampton Ct. DE56 16 F3
Bridge Foot. DE56 16 B3
Bridge Hill. DE56 16 A3
Bridge St. DE56 16 B3
Bridge View. DE56 17 C8
Brookside. DE56 16 B4
Broom Clo. DE56 16 A2
Browns La. DE56 17 F8
Bullsmoor. DE56 16 E3
Burbage Clo. DE56 16 F3
Calver Clo. DE56 16 D2
Campbell St. DE56 16 B4
Canada St. DE56 17 C5
Cedar Gro. DE56 17 D5
Cemetery Rd. DE56 16 C2
Chapel St, Belper. DE56 16 B4
Chapel St, Holbrook Moor. DE56 17 E8
Charnwood Av. DE56 16 C3
Cheapside. DE56 16 B4
Cherry Tree Av. DE56 16 D1
Chesterfield Rd, Belper. DE56 16 C4
Chesterfield Rd, Far Laund. DE56 16 D1
Chestnut Av, Cowhill. DE56 17 C5
Chestnut Av, Holbrook Moor. DE56 17 E8
Chevin Rd. DE56 17 A5
Chevin View. DE56 16 B4
Church La. DE56 16 C4
Cluster Rd. DE56 16 B3
Coronation Av. DE56 16 C2
Courtney Way. DE56 16 F3
Crich La. DE56 16 C1
*Crown Ter, Bridge St. DE56 16 B3
Culworth Clo. DE56 16 F3
Dark La. DE56 17 D8
Days La. DE56 16 B4
Deepdale Rd. DE56 16 D3
Derby Rd. DE56 17 B5
Derwent Av. DE56 17 C7
Derwent St. DE56 16 B4
Derwent Vale. DE56 17 B5
Dovedale Cres. DE56 16 D3
Duncan Clo. DE56 16 D2
East Cres. DE56 17 E7
East Ter. DE56 17 C8
Edale Way. DE56 16 C3
Edensor Way. DE56 16 E1
Edward St. DE56 16 C3
Elm Av. DE56 17 D5
*Eyam Walk, Acorn Dri. DE56 16 C3
Falcons Rise. DE56 16 E2
Far Laund. DE56 16 D2
Farm Clo. DE56 16 E3
Fellside. DE56 16 C3
Field La. DE56 16 B4
Findern Clo. DE56 16 D2
Fleet Cres. DE56 17 C5
Fleet Park. DE56 16 C4
Ford St. DE56 16 C3
Forest Clo. DE56 16 D2
Foundry La. DE56 17 B8
George St. DE56 16 B3
Gibfield La. DE56 17 B5
Glen Av. DE56 17 E8
Glen View. DE56 17 C5
Goods Rd. DE56 17 B5
Gorsey Rd. DE56 16 A2
Grangewood Dri. DE56 17 C8
Green La. DE56 16 B3
Gregorys Way. DE56 16 E2
Harrier Rd. DE56 16 E2
Hayfield Clo. DE56 16 D2
Heydon Clo. DE56 16 E2
*High Edge Mews, Acorn Dri. DE56 16 C3
High Pavement. DE56 16 C4
High St. DE56 16 C4
Highfield Rd. DE56 17 C5
Highwood Av. DE56 17 E6
Hillside Rise. DE56 17 B5
Holbrook Rd. DE56 17 B5
Honeycroft Clo. DE56 17 D5
Hopping Hill. DE56 17 B7
Horsley Cres. DE56 17 E8
Hunters Rd. DE56 16 F3
INDUSTRIAL ESTATES:
Goods Rd Ind Est. DE56 17 B5
Ingles Channel. DE56 16 C3
Jacksons La, Far Laund. DE56 16 F1
Jacksons La, Milford. DE56 17 A7
Joddrell Av. DE56 16 F4
John O'Gaunts Way. DE56 16 E3
Joseph St. DE56 16 B3
Jubilee Ct. DE56 17 C5
Kilburn La. DE56 16 F4
Kilburn Rd. DE56 16 E3
Killis La. DE56 17 E7
King St. DE56 16 B4
Kirks La. DE56 16 D4
Knowl Av. DE56 16 A2
*Ladywell Ct, Alder Rd. DE56 17 C5
Ladywood Av. DE56 16 D2
Lander La. DE56 16 C4
Laund Av. DE56 16 D2
Laund Clo. DE56 16 D2
Laund Hill. DE56 16 C3
Laund Nook. DE56 16 D3
Laund Nook Rd. DE56 16 C3
Leche Croft. DE56 16 F3
*Leycote Way, Allstone Lee. DE56 16 B3
Lime Cres. DE56 17 D5
Litton Clo. DE56 16 D3
Lodge Dri. DE56 16 A2
Long Row. DE56 16 B3
Longstone Rise. DE56 16 D1
Lowlands Rd. DE56 16 D3
Makeney Rd, Milford. DE56 17 C8
Makeney Rd, Holbrook Moor. DE56 17 E8
Manor Rd. DE56 16 B4
Maple Dri. DE56 17 D5
Market Pl. DE56 16 C4
Marlborough Dri. DE56 16 E3
Marsh La. DE56 16 C3
Marsh La Cres. DE56 16 D3
Marston Clo. DE56 16 E1
Martindale Ct. DE56 16 F2
Matlock Rd. DE56 16 B1
Meadow Ct. DE56 16 B4
Meadow View. DE56 17 B5
Melbourne Clo. DE56 17 C5
Merlin Clo. DE56 16 E2
Mill La. DE56 16 D4
Mill St. DE56 16 B3
Milldale Ct. DE56 17 D5
Millersdale Clo. DE56 16 E3
Monyash Way. DE56 16 D2
Moor Rise. DE56 17 E8
Moorfield Rd. DE56 17 E8
Moorpool Cres. DE56 17 E8
Moorside La. DE56 17 E7
Morrel Wood Dri. DE56 16 F2
Moulton Clo. DE56 16 F3
Mount Pleasant Dri. DE56 16 A2
Mulberry Clo. DE56 17 D5
Nailers Way. DE56 16 E2
Naseby Rd. DE56 16 F3
New Breck Rd. DE56 16 C4
New Rd, Belper. DE56 16 B4
New Rd, Far Laund. DE56 16 E1
Norbury Way. DE56 16 E1
North La. DE56 17 A7
Nottingham Rd. DE56 16 C4
Oakhurst Clo. DE56 16 A2
Over La. DE56 16 F4
*Overstone Clo, Naseby Rd. DE56 16 F3
Park Rd. DE56 17 D5
Parkside. DE56 16 C4
Penn St. DE56 16 C3
Pilsley Clo. DE56 16 E2
Pinchoms Hill Rd. DE56 17 D5
Pinewood Rd. DE56 16 A2
Pingle Cres. DE56 16 B3
Pingle La. DE56 16 B3
Pond Rd. DE56 17 E8
Pottery Clo. DE56 16 E2
Primary Clo. DE56 16 C4
Prospect Dri. DE56 17 B5
Pytchley Clo. DE56 16 F3
Quarry Rd. DE56 17 B6
Queen St. DE56 16 C4
Queens Dri. DE56 16 A2
Raven Oak Clo. DE56 17 C5
Rothwell La. DE56 16 D4
Royal Gate. DE56 16 F4
Ruffstone Clo. DE56 17 E8
Ryegrass Clo. DE56 16 F4
St James Clo. DE56 16 F3
St Johns Rd. DE56 16 C4
St Peters Clo. DE56 16 C4
Sandbed La. DE56 16 F4
Shaw La. DE56 17 B7
Shireoaks. DE56 16 A2
Short Row. DE56 16 B3
Short St. DE56 16 E3
Shortlands. DE56 16 C4
Snowberry Av. DE56 17 D5
Spencer Av. DE56 16 D3
Spencer Rd. DE56 16 C3
Spinners Way. DE56 16 E2
Spring Clo. DE56 16 A2
Stanton Av. DE56 16 D4
Stoke Clo. DE56 16 F3
Strutt St. DE56 16 B4
Sunny Bank Gdns. DE56 17 B5
Sunny Hill. DE56 17 B8
Swinney Bank. DE56 16 C3
Swinney La. DE56 16 C3
The Avenue. DE56 17 B5
The Butts. DE56 16 C4
The Croft. DE56 17 E6
The Fleet. DE56 16 C4
The Green. DE56 16 C2
The Hawthorns. DE56 16 F3
The Nook. DE56 17 E8
The Orchard. DE56 16 C3
The Pinfold. DE56 16 F2
The Scotches. DE56 16 B2
The Spinney. DE56 16 C2
Thorpe Way. DE56 16 D2
Valley Vw. DE56 17 C5
Vicarage Clo. DE56 16 C4
Vicarage Rd. DE56 17 C7
Vicarwood Av. DE56 17 E8
Walcote Clo. DE56 16 E2
Walnut Rd. DE56 17 D5
Weavers Clo. DE56 16 E2
Well La. DE56 17 B8
Wellington Ct. DE56 16 B4
Westbury Gdns. DE56 16 E3
Wheeldon Av. DE56 16 D3
Whitehouse Rise. DE56 16 A2
Whitemoor La. DE56 16 E3
Wicksteed. DE56 16 F3
Wilders Lea Ct. DE56 17 C6
William St. DE56 16 B3
Willow Gro. DE56 17 C5
Wilmot Rd. DE56 16 C4
Windmill La. DE56 16 C3
Windmill Rise. DE56 16 C3
Winster Clo. DE56 16 D2
Wood La. DE56 17 B8
Wren Park Clo. DE56 16 A2
Wyver La. DE56 16 A1
Yardley Way. DE56 16 F3

BOLSOVER

Avondale Rd. S44 18 C3
Bainbridge Rd. S44 18 B3
Bank Clo. S44 18 C1
Bathurst Rd. S44 18 A3
Beck Clo. S44 18 E2
Blind La. S44 18 A1
Bretton Av. S44 18 E2
Brookfield Rd. S44 18 C3
Carr Vale Rd. S44 18 B3
Castle Green. S44 18 D4
Castle La. S44 18 B3
Castle St. S44 18 C2
Cavendish Rd. S44 18 D3
Cavendish Walk. S44 18 C2
Cedar Park Dri. S44 18 E2
Chapel Rd. S44 18 B3
Charlesworth St. S44 18 A3
Chatsworth Clo. S44 18 E2
Cherry Tree Clo. S44 18 D2
Chesterfield Rd. S44 18 A2
Church St. S44 18 C3
Conduit Rd. S44 18 C3
Cornmill Clo. S44 18 D2
Cotton St. S44 18 C2
Crich View. S44 18 D4
Cromwell Rd. S44 18 D3
Cross St. S44 18 D4
Cundy Rd. S44 18 B1
Darwood La. S44 18 C4
Davey Ct. S44 18 B1
Deepdale Rd. S44 18 B1
Dumbles Rd. S44 18 B3
Dykes Clo. S44 18 C2
Eastern Av. S44 18 D4
Elm Clo. S44 18 E3
Elmton La. S44 18 D2
Fairfield Rd. S44 18 C3
Farmfields Clo. S44 18 A1
Greenway Dri. S44 18 B3
Haldane Cres. S44 18 B1
Harvey Ct. S44 18 B1
Haslam Ct. S44 18 B2
Hides Grn. S44 18 C2
High St. S44 18 C2
Highfield Rd. S44 18 C3
Hill Top. S44 18 C1
Holbeck Av. S44 18 E2
Hornscroft Rd. S44 18 C3
Horsehead La. S44 18 D2
Houfton Cres. S44 18 A1
Houfton Rd. S44 18 A1
Houldsworth Cres. S44 18 B1
Hudson Mnt. S44 18 D4
Huntingdon Av. S44 18 D3
Hyndley Rd. S44 18 B1
INDUSTRIAL ESTATES:
Bolsover Enterprise Park. S44 18 A1
Iron Cliffe Rd. S44 18 B1
Kitchen Croft. S44 18 C2
Laburnum Clo. S44 18 D3
Langstone Av. S44 18 E3
Langwith Rd. S44 18 C3
Lilac Gro. S44 18 E3
Limekiln Fields Rd. S44 18 C1
Longlands. S44 18 C2
Lords Clo. S44 18 C3
Main St. S44 18 A4
Manor Court Rd. S44 18 B1
Mansfield Rd. S44 18 D4
Market Pl. S44 18 C2
Marlpit La. S44 18 D2
Meadow Clo. S44 18 C3
Meadowlands. S44 18 E2
Middle St. S44 18 C2
Middle St, Hillstown. S44 18 E4
Mill La. S44 18 C1
Mill Walk. S44 18 C1
Moor La. S44 18 D3
Mooracre La. S44 18 E3
Moorfield Av. S44 18 D3
Moorfield Sq. S44 18 D3
Morven Av. S44 18 D3
Nesbit St. S44 18 D4
Nethersprings Rd. S44 18 B1
New Station Rd. S44 18 B3
New St. S44 18 C1
North View St. S44 18 A3
Old Hill. S44 18 B2
Orchard Clo. S44 18 D2
Orchard View. S44 18 A4
Ovencroft La. S44 18 E1
Owlcotes View. S44 18 C4
Oxcroft La. S44 18 C1
*Pegasus Ct, Welbeck Rd. S44 18 C2
Pevervil Rd. S44 18 B1
Pleasant Av. S44 18 D4
Polyfields La. S44 18 D4
Portland Av. S44 18 D3
Portland Cres. S44 18 D3
Quarry Rd. S44 18 C1
Redacre Clo. S44 18 D2
Ridgedale Rd. S44 18 C3
Ridgeway Av. S44 18 D2
Rosehill Ct. S44 18 B3
Rotherham Rd. S44 18 F4
Rutland Av. S44 18 B3
St Lawrence Av. S44 18 D3
Sandhills Rd. S44 18 D3
Scarsdale St. S44 18 A4
Searson Av. S44 18 C3
Selwyn St. S44 18 D4
Sherwood St. S44 18 A3
Shuttlewood Rd. S44 18 C1
Smithson Av. S44 18 D3
South Cres. S44 18 D3
Spencer St. S44 18 B3
Spittal Grn. S44 18 C3
Springfield Cres. S44 18 B1
Stables Ct. S44 18 E3
Station Rd. S44 18 A2
Steel La. S44 18 D2
Stockley View. S44 18 D4
Stratton Rd. S44 18 C1
Surprise Walk. S44 18 C3
Sutton Hall Rd. S44 18 A4
Sutton View. S44 18 D4
Sycamore Clo. S44 18 E2
The Paddock. S44 18 D2
Tower Cres. S44 18 D3
Town End. S44 18 C2
Vale Clo. S44 18 B3
Valley Rd. S44 18 B3
Victoria St. S44 18 D4
Villas Rd. S44 18 A2
Welbeck Rd. S44 18 C2
Wells St. S44 18 E4
West View. S44 18 D4
Windmill Clo. S44 18 C1
Woodhouse La. S44 18 A1
Woodhouse Rd. S44 18 B2

BUXTON

Alder Gro. SK17 20 B2
Aldwark Rd. SK17 21 D5
Alexandra Rd. SK17 21 D5
Alma St. SK17 20 E2
Alport Av. SK17 20 E3
Alsop Gro,. SK17 20 F4
Alsop Pl. SK17 20 F4
Alsop Way. SK17 20 F4
Amberley Dri. SK17 21 E5
Arbor Gro. SK17 20 A4
Ash St. SK17 20 C4
Ash Ter. SK17 20 D2
Ashbourne Rd. SK17 21 D5
Ashwood Clo. SK17 20 D4
Ashwood Rd. SK17 20 F2
Aspen Clo. SK17 20 C2
B Road Walk. SK17 20 C4
Bailey Gro. SK17 20 F3
Bakewell Rd. SK17 20 E3
Barms Way. SK17 20 E2
Barson Gro. SK17 21 F8
Baslow Gro. SK17 20 F4
Bath Rd. SK17 20 C4
Bench Rd. SK17 20 E2
Bennett St. SK17 20 D4
Berwick Rd. SK17 21 E6
Birch Clo. SK17 20 C2

Bishops La. SK17 20 A4
Boarstones La. SK17 20 F3
Bridge St. SK17 20 D2
Brooklands. SK17 20 D2
Brown Edge Rd. SK17 20 D2
Burlington Rd. SK17 20 C3
Burlow Av. SK17 21 E7
Burlow Rd. SK17 21 E7
Byron St. SK17 20 D4
Calesdale Clo. SK17 21 D5
Carlisle Gro. SK17 20 B3
Carlisle Rd. SK17 20 B3
Cavendish Av. SK17 20 A4
Central St. SK17 21 E5
Chapel St. SK17 20 C4
Charles St. SK17 20 D2
Chatsworth Rd. SK17 20 F4
Cheedale. SK17 20 E3
Cherrytree Dri. SK17 20 F2
Chestnut Clo. SK17 20 C2
Church St. SK17 20 C4
Cliff Rd. SK17 20 E2
Clifton Bank. SK17 20 E2
Clifton Dri. SK17 21 E5
Clifton Rd. SK17 20 D3
Clough St. SK17 20 C4
College Rd. SK17 20 C4
Compton Gro. SK17 20 C4
Compton Rd. SK17 20 C4
Corbar Rd. SK17 20 C2
Corbar Woods La.
  SK17 20 C2
Cornwall Av. SK17 20 F3
*Crich Pl,
  Granby Rd. SK17 20 E3
*Cromford La,
  Granby Rd. SK17 20 E3
*Cromford Pl,
  Granby Rd. SK17 20 E3
Cross St. SK17 20 D4
Crowestones. SK17 20 D4
Cumberland Clo. SK17 21 E6
Curzon St. SK17 20 D3
Dakin Av. SK17 20 E2
Dale La. SK17 20 F2
Dale Rd. SK17 20 D4
Dale Side. SK17 20 D4
Dane Gro. SK17 21 D6
Darley Gro. SK17 20 F4
*Darley Way,
  Granby Rd. SK17 20 E3
Darwin Av. SK17 20 D3
Derwent Rd. SK17 21 D5
Devonshire Rd. SK17 20 C2
Dew Pond La. SK17 21 F8
Dolby Rd. SK17 21 F8
Dorset Clo. SK17 21 E6
Dovedale Cres. SK17 20 A4
Doveridge Gro. SK17 20 A4
Duke St. SK17 20 A4
Dukes Dri. SK17 20 E4
Eagle Par. SK17 20 E4
Ecclesbourne Dri. SK17 20 B4
*Edale Gro,
  Kinder Way. SK17 20 F4
*Edale Way,
  Granby Rd. SK17 20 F4
Edensor Av. SK17 20 F3
Elizabeth Av. SK17 20 F3
Elton Gro. SK17 20 F4
Errwood Av. SK17 20 B4
Fairfield Rd. SK17 20 C4
Fern Rd. SK17 21 D5
Ferneydale Av. SK17 21 D6
Fernway. SK17 21 D7
Fiddle St. SK17 21 D7
Forest Av. SK17 20 D4
Fountain St. SK17 20 C3
Foxes Yd. SK17 20 F2
Foxlow Av. SK17 21 D6
Friar Gro. SK17 20 D4
Gadley La. SK17 20 A3
Glebe Rd. SK17 20 E3
Glenmoor Rd. SK17 20 E2
Goytlands. SK17 20 B4
Granby Rd. SK17 20 E3
Grange Rd. SK17 20 D4
Green La. SK17 20 A4
Gretton Rd. SK17 20 E3
Grin Low Rd. SK17 21 A6
Grinlow Clo. SK17 21 D7
Grove St. SK17 21 E5
Haddon Rd. SK17 20 C3
Hall Bank. SK17 20 C3
Hardwick Mnt. SK17 20 D3

Hardwick Sq East.
  SK17 20 D3
Hardwick Sq Nth.
  SK17 20 D3
Hardwick Sq Sth.
  SK17 20 D3
Hardwick St. SK17 20 D3
Hargate Rd. SK17 20 B4
Harpur Hill Rd. SK17 21 D5
Harris Rd. SK17 21 E7
Hartington Rd. SK17 20 C4
Haslin Rd. SK17 21 E8
Hastings Rd. SK17 21 E6
Heath Gro. SK17 20 D3
Heath Park Rd. SK17 20 D4
Heath St. SK17 20 D4
Heathfield Nook Rd.
  SK17 21 F8
Hereford Clo. SK17 21 E6
Hereford Rd. SK17 21 E5
High St. SK17 20 C4
Highlands Clo. SK17 21 D5
Hillside. SK17 21 F7
Hogshaw Vs Rd. SK17 20 D2
Holker Av. SK17 20 D3
Holker Rd. SK17 20 D3
Hollins St. SK17 20 C4
Holmfield. SK17 20 A4
INDUSTRIAL ESTATES:
  Staden Business Pk.
  SK17 21 F6
Kedleston Rd. SK17 20 D4
Kelsons Av. SK17 21 E5
Kendal Clo. SK17 21 E5
Kents Bank Rd. SK17 20 D4
Kinder Gro. SK17 20 B4
Kinder Way. SK17 20 F4
Kings Clo. SK17 20 F2
Kings Rd. SK17 20 E3
Kirkstone Rd. SK17 21 E7
Knowles Clo. SK17 20 F2
Knowles Cres. SK17 20 F2
Ladycroft Av. SK17 20 D2
Lansdowne Rd. SK17 20 C2
Lascelles Rd. SK17 20 C2
Lathkil Gro. SK17 20 E3
Lee Dale. SK17 21 D7
Lightwood Rd. SK17 20 C1
Lismore Gro. SK17 20 B4
Lismore Park. SK17 20 B4
Lismore Rd. SK17 20 B4
London Rd. SK17 20 D4
Macclesfield Rd. SK17 20 A4
Manchester Rd. SK17 20 A1
Market Pl. SK17 20 C3
Market St. SK17 20 D4
Marlborough Rd. SK17 20 C2
Marlow St. SK17 20 D4
Mill Cliff. SK17 20 D3
Milldale Av. SK17 20 E4
Millersdale Way. SK17 21 C5
Milnbank Av. SK17 20 E3
Monsal Av. SK17 20 E3
Monsal Gro. SK17 20 E3
Montpelier Pl. SK17 20 F2
Mosley St. SK17 20 F2
Nettleton La. SK17 21 E7
New High St. SK17 20 E2
New Market St. SK17 20 D4
Newstead Ter. SK17 20 D4
Nicholas Clo. SK17 20 F3
Nunbrook Gro. SK17 20 D2
Nunsfield Rd. SK17 20 E2
Nursery Dri. SK17 20 D1
Nursery La. SK17 20 A4
Oaklea. SK17 21 D5
Overdale Av. SK17 20 C3
Palace Rd. SK17 20 D2
Park Rd. SK17 20 B2
Peveril Rd. SK17 20 D4
Pictor Gro. SK17 20 E4
Pictor Rd. SK17 20 E4
Princes St. SK17 20 E2
Queens Av. SK17 20 E2
Queens Rd. SK17 20 E2
Railway Ter. SK17 20 D2
Ripon Gdns. SK17 21 E6
Robertson Rd. SK17 20 C4
Rock Bank. SK17 21 D7
Rock Ter. SK17 20 C4
Rockfield Rd. SK17 20 E2
St James St. SK17 20 C4
St James Ter. SK17 20 C4
St Johns Rd. SK17 20 A4

St Peters Rd. SK17 20 E2
Sheraton Way. SK17 20 C2
Sherbrook Gro. SK17 21 D5
Sherwood Rd. SK17 21 D5
Silverlands. SK17 20 D3
Silverlands Clo. SK17 20 E3
Silverlands Park. SK17 20 D3
Solomns Vw. SK17 20 D4
Somerset Clo. SK17 21 E5
South Av. SK17 20 D3
South St. SK17 20 C4
Spencer Gro. SK17 20 C4
Spencer Rd. SK17 20 C4
Spring Gdns. SK17 20 D3
Staden La. SK17 21 F6
Station Rd. SK17 20 C3
*Stonecliffe Ter,
  Victoria Pk Rd. SK17 20 E3
Sycamore Clo. SK17 20 C2
Sylvan Cliff. SK17 20 D4
Tedder Av. SK17 21 E7
Temple Rd. SK17 20 B4
Temple View. SK17 20 D4
Terrace Rd. SK17 20 D3
The Crescent. SK17 20 C3
The Glade. SK17 20 B3
The Paddock. SK17 20 B3
The Quadrant. SK17 20 D3
The Square. SK17 20 C3
Thorn Clo. SK17 20 F3
Thornsett Av. SK17 20 F3
Tongue La. SK17 20 F2
Torr St. SK17 20 C4
Town End. SK17 20 F2
Trenchard St. SK17 21 E7
Trent Av. SK17 21 D6
Turncliffe Clo. SK17 20 B4
Valerian Clo. SK17 20 E4
Victoria Park Rd. SK17 20 E3
Wall St. SK17 20 E2
Water St. SK17 20 C3
Waterwallows Rd.
  SK17 20 E1
Watford Rd. SK17 20 B3
Welbeck Av. SK17 21 D5
West Rd. SK17 20 C4
White Knowle Pk.
  SK17 21 D5
White Knowle Rd.
  SK17 21 D5
Williamson Av. SK17 20 D2
Windsor Pk Rd. SK17 20 E2
Windsor Rd. SK17 20 E2
Winster Gro. SK17 20 F4
Winster Sq.. SK17 20 F4
Woodside Gdns. SK17 20 E3
Wye Gro. SK17 20 B4
Wye St. SK17 20 D3
Wyedale Clo. SK17 21 D5
Wyehead Clo. SK17 20 B4
Wyelands Clo. SK17 20 B4

CHAPEL-EN-LE-FRITH

Alston Rd. SK12 19 C4
Anchor Av. SK12 19 E3
Anchor Fold. SK12 19 E3
Ashbourne Rd. SK12 19 E3
Ashfield Rd SK12 19 E3
Bagshawe Av. SK12 19 B3
Bank Hall Dri. SK12 19 C4
Barlow Rd. SK12 19 D3
Beresford Av. SK12 19 E3
Beresford Rd. SK12 19 E3
Blackbrook Rd. SK12 19 F3
Bowden Head La.
  SK12 19 E1
Bowden La. SK12 19 D2
Bridgeway. SK12 19 D4
Brooklands Av. SK12 19 E3
Brooklands Rd. SK12 19 E3
Brookside Rd. SK12 19 D4
Burdekin Clo. SK12 19 E3
Burrfields Rd. SK12 19 D3
Buxton Rd. SK12 19 E3
Castleton Rd. SK12 19 E3
Charley La. SK12 19 A2
Church Brow. SK12 19 C2
Church La. SK12 19 C2
Cromwell Av. SK12 19 C4
Cross St. SK12 19 C3
Crossings Av. SK12 19 B3

Crossings Rd. SK12 19 A3
Danes Way. SK12 19 D2
Downlee Clo. SK12 19 B4
Drum and Monkey.
  SK12 19 C1
Eastbrook Clo. SK12 19 D3
Eaves Av. SK12 19 D3
Eccles Fold. SK12 19 B3
Eccles Rd. SK12 19 A2
Eldon Clo. SK12 19 E3
Elmfield. SK12 19 B4
Fern Bank. SK12 19 D2
Frith View. SK12 19 B4
Gisborne Dri. SK12 19 C4
Grange Park Av. SK12 19 D4
Grange Park Rd. SK12 19 D3
Grange Av. SK12 19 C4
Green Park Av. SK12 19 D3
Greggs. SK12 19 B4
Hall Hill. SK12 19 A1
Hawthorne Rd. SK12 19 C4
Hayfield St. SK12 19 C4
Hayfield Rd East. SK12 19 D2
Heyworth Rd. SK12 19 D3
High St. SK12 19 C3
Higher Crossings.
  SK12 19 A2
Hollin Dri. SK12 19 C4
Hordens La. SK12 19 C4
Hordens Park Rd.
  SK12 19 C4
Hordens Rd. SK12 19 C3
Horsefair Av. SK12 19 B3
Johnson Way. SK12 19 E3
Jubilee Rd. SK12 19 C3
Knowle Av. SK12 19 C4
Laneside Clo. SK12 19 C4
Lee Field Rd. SK12 19 C4
Links Rd. SK12 19 B4
Long La. SK12 19 B3
Longmeade Dri. SK12 19 E3
Longson Rd. SK12 19 E3
Lower Eaves View.
  SK12 19 D3
Manchester Rd. SK12 19 A4
Market Pl. SK12 19 C3
Market St. SK12 19 D3
Marsh Hall La. SK12 19 A4
Mellor La. SK12 19 B3
Midland Rd. SK12 19 C3
Moss View Rd. SK12 19 D3
Nearwell Clo. SK12 19 B3
Netherfield Rd. SK12 19 E3
Oak Clo. SK12 19 D4
Old School Yd. SK12 19 D3
Park Cres. SK12 19 D3
Park Rd. SK12 19 D3
Park View Dri. SK12 19 D3
Pickford Pl. SK12 19 C3
Pleaslows. SK12 19 F3
Poplar Ter. SK12 19 D2
Quentin Rd. SK12 19 D3
Reddish Grn. SK12 19 E3
Roebuck Pl. SK12 19 C3
Rowton Grange Rd.
  SK12 19 C3
St Anns Clo. SK12 19 B3
*Sandyway Head,
  Buxton Rd. SK12 19 E3
Sheffield Rd. SK12 19 F2
Spencer Rd. SK12 19 B3
Station Dri. SK12 19 C4
Station Rd. SK12 19 C3
Stockport Rd. SK12 19 A1
Sycamore Rd. SK12 19 C4
Terrace Rd. SK12 19 C3
The Crescent. SK12 19 D2
Thornbrook Rd. SK12 19 D3
Thornell Clo. SK12 19 E3
Warmbrook Rd. SK12 19 D3
Westbrook Clo. SK12 19 D3
Willow Dri. SK12 19 D4
Wilshaw Clo. SK12 19 E3
Woodbine Ter. SK12 19 C3
Woodlands Rd. SK12 19 C4

CHESTERFIELD CENTRE

Abercrombie St. S41 22 C3
*Acres View Clo,
  Highfield La. S41 22 A1
Albion Rd. S40 22 B4

Alexandra Rd West.
  S40 22 B4
Alma St West. S40 22 B5
Ashdown Dri. S40 22 A6
Ashgate Rd. S40 22 A3
Ashgate Valley Rd. S40 22 A3
Aspley Clo. S40 22 A2
Avondale Rd. S40 22 B3
Baden Powell Av. S40 22 C6
Baden Powell Rd. S40 22 C5
Bank Rd. S41 22 C1
Bank St. S40 22 B4
Barbon Clo. S40 22 A2
Barker Fold. S40 22 A4
Barker La. S40 22 A4
Basil Clo. S41 22 D4
Beaver Pl. S40 22 A5
Beechdale Clo. S40 22 A2
Beehive Rd. S40 22 A4
Beehive Yard. S40 22 A5
Beetwell St. S40 22 C5
Bentham Rd. S40 22 A2
Boythorpe Av. S40 22 B5
Boythorpe Cres. S40 22 B6
Boythorpe Mnt. S40 22 B6
Boythorpe Rise. S40 22 A5
Boythorpe Rd. S41 22 B4
Bramshill Rise. S40 22 A6
Branton Clo. S40 22 B6
Brent Clo. S40 22 A2
Brewery St. S41 22 D4
Briar Clo. S41 22 A2
Brickhouse Yard. S40 22 A4
Brickyard Walk. S40 22 C3
Bridge St. S40 22 D6
Brimington Rd. S41 22 D4
Brindley Rd. S41 22 C1
*Broad Pavement,
  Knifesmithgate. S40 22 C4
Brockwell La. S40 22 A2
Brockwell Pl. S40 22 A3
Brockwell Ter. S40 22 A3
Brook Vale. S40 22 A5
Brook Yard. S40 22 B4
Brookbank Av. S40 22 A3
Brooklyn Dri. S40 22 A3
Brunswick St. S41 22 C3
Buckden Clo. S40 22 A3
Burlington St. S40 22 C4
Byron St. S40 22 D6
Cambrian Clo. S40 22 A1
Canal Wharf. S41 22 D3
Catherines St. S40 22 B4
Cavendish St. S40 22 C4
Cedar Av. S40 22 A2
Central Av. S40 22 B5
Central Ter. S40 22 D5
Chantrey Av. S41 22 C1
Charles St. S40 22 A4
Chatsworth Rd. S40 22 A5
Chester St. S40 22 A4
Church La. S40 22 C4
Church Wk. S40 22 D4
Church Way. S40 22 D4
Clarence Rd. S40 22 B4
Clarence St. S40 22 B4
Clarkson Av. S40 22 C6
Clayton St. S40 22 D5
Clifton St. S40 22 A4
Clubmill Ter. S40 22 A3
Cobden Rd. S40 22 B3
Compton St. S40 22 B3
Craven Rd. S41 22 B2
Cromwell Rd. S40 22 B3
Cross St. S40 22 B3
Crow La. S41 22 D4
Crown Rd. S41 22 C1
Darwin Clo. S40 22 B3
Darwin Rd. S40 22 B3
Derby Rd. S40 22 D6
Dixon Rd. S41 22 D5
Dock Walk. S40 22 B5
Dowdeswell St. S41 22 C3
Dukes Dri. S41 22 A1
Dundonald Rd. S40 22 C6
Durrant Rd. S41 22 D4
Edinburgh Rd. S41 22 B2
Elder Way. S40 22 C4
Elton St. S40 22 C5
Enfield Rd. S41 22 C2
Eyre Gdns. S41 22 B2
Factory St. S40 22 A5
Fair Clo. S40 22 A3
Fairfield Rd. S40 22 B3
Farnon Clo. S40 22 D6

58

Flamsteed Cres. S41 22 C1
Foljambe Rd. S40 22 B4
Foolow Av. S40 22 B6
Franklyn Rd. S40 22 A3
Glade Clo. S40 22 A2
Gladstone Rd. S40 22 B3
Gloucester Av. S41 22 B2
Gloucester Rd. S41 22 B2
Glumangate. S40 22 C4
Goyt Side Rd. S40 22 A5
Grindlow Av. S40 22 B6
Hady Hill. S41 22 D5
Hall View. S41 22 B1
Hardwick St. S41 22 C3
Hardwicks Yard. S40 22 A5
Hartside Clo. S40 22 A2
Hasland By-Pass. S41 22 D6
Hasland St. S41 22 D6
Hastings Clo. S41 22 A1
Hawkesley Av. S40 22 B2
Hawthorne St. S40 22 D6
Hazel Dri. S40 22 A6
Hazlehurst Av. S40 22 D2
Hazlehurst La. S41 22 D2
Heathfield Av. S40 22 A4
Herriot Dri. S40 22 D6
High St. S40 22 C4
Highbury Rd. S41 22 B2
Higher Albert St. S41 22 C3
Highfield Av. S41 22 A1
Highfield St. S41 22 A1
Highfield Rd. S41 22 A1
Highfield View Rd. S41 22 C1
Hipper St. S40 22 D5
Hipper St Sth. S40 22 C5
Hipper St West. S40 22 A5
Holbeck Clo. S41 22 D3
Hollis La. S41 22 D4
Holme Rd. S41 22 C1
Holmebank Clo. S40 22 A3
Holmebank East. S40 22 A3
Holmebank View. S40 22 A3
Holmebank West. S40 22 A3
Holywell. S41 22 C4
Homeport Mews. S41 22 C3
Hope St. S40 22 A4
Hucklow Av. S40 22 B6
Hunloke Av. S40 22 A6
Hunloke Cres. S40 22 A6
Infirmary Rd. S41 22 D3
Inner Relief Rd. S41 22 D1
James St. S41 22 D1
John St. S40 22 A4
Johnstone Clo. S40 22 C6
Keilder Ct. S40 22 A6
Kennet Vale. S40 22 A2
Kent Clo. S41 22 C2
Kingsmede Av. S40 22 A6
Knifesmithgate. S40 22 C4
Lansdowne Av. S41 22 A1
Larch Way. S40 22 A2
Leyburn Clo. S40 22 A2
Linden Park Gro. S40 22 A4
Lockerfold La. S41 22 C1
Lockoford Rd. S41 22 C1
Lord Roberts Rd. S40 22 C6
Lordsmill St. S41 22 D5
Low Pavement. S40 22 C4
Lower Grove Rd. S40 22 B4
Lucas Rd. S41 22 B1
Madin St. S41 22 C3
Malham Clo. S40 22 A2
Malson Way. S41 22 C1
Malt House Ct. S41 22 C3
Malvern Rd. S40 22 B3
Mansfeldt Cres. S41 22 B1
Mansfeldt Rd. S41 22 B1
Marchwood Clo. S40 22 B3
*Market Pl,
  High St. S40 22 C4
Markham Rd. S40 22 B4
Marsden Pl. S40 22 A5
Marsden Pl. S40 22 C3
Marsden St. S40 22 C4
Maynard Rd. S40 22 C6
Mill La. S40 22 A5
Mill St. S41 22 D4
Minimum Ter. S40 22 B5
Morris Av. S41 22 B2
Morris Dri. S41 22 B2
Mound Rd. S40 22 C6
Nelson St. S41 22 C1
New Beetwell St. S40 22 C4
New Queen St. S41 22 C3

*New Sq,
  High St. S40 22 C4
New St. S40 22 C5
Newbold Av. S41 22 A1
Newbold Back La. S40 22 A2
Newbold Dri. S41 22 A1
Newbold Rd. S41 22 A1
Newland Dri. S41 22 C2
Newland Gdns. S41 22 B2
Oakley Av. S40 22 B3
Old Hall Rd. S40 22 A4
Old Rd. S40 22 A5
Outram St. S41 22 C1
Packers Row. S40 22 C4
Park Rd. S40 22 C5
Parkers Yard. S41 22 D4
Pevensey Av. S41 22 B1
Peveril Rd. S41 22 C1
Pond St. S40 22 C5
Princess St. S41 22 C3
Prospect Ter. S40 22 A3
Purbeck Av. S40 22 A3
Queen St. S40 22 C3
Ramsey Av. S40 22 A6
Redvers Buller Rd. S40 22 C6
Reservoir Ter. S40 22 B3
Rhodes Av. S41 22 A2
Riber Ter. S40 22 B5
Ringwood Av. S41 22 D1
Rose Hill. S40 22 C4
Rose Hill East. S40 22 C4
Rose Hill West. S40 22 C4
Rother Way. S41 22 D1
Rufford Clo. S40 22 B6
Rutland Rd. S40 22 B4
St Augustines Av. S40 22 C6
St Augustines Dri. S40 22 C6
St Augustines Mount.
  S40 22 C6
St Helens Clo. S41 22 C3
St Helens St. S41 22 C3
St Margarets Dri. S40 22 B4
St Marks Rd. S40 22 A4
St Marys Gate. S41 22 D4
Salcey Sq. S40 22 A6
Saltergate. S40 22 B4
Sanforth St. S41 22 C1
School Board La. S40 22 A4
Selhurst Rd. S41 22 B2
Shaftesbury Av. S40 22 A4
Sheffield Rd. S41 22 C1
Shepley St. S40 22 A5
Sherwood St. S40 22 D6
Shirland St. S41 22 C3
Sitwell Av. S40 22 B6
Soresby St. S40 22 C4
South Pl,
  Brampton. S40 22 A4
South Pl,
  Chesterfield. S40 22 C5
Spa La. S41 22 D4
Spencer St. S40 22 C3
*Spring Pl,
  Brickyard Wk. S40 22 C3
Springbank Rd. S40 22 B4
Springfield Av. S40 22 A4
Station Rd. S41 22 D4
Stephenson Pl. S40 22 D4
Sterland St. S41 22 A4
Stone Row. S40 22 A5
Stonegravels La. S41 22 D2
Summerfield Rd. S40 22 B6
Sunnysprings. S41 22 C3
Sycamore Av. S40 22 A6
Sydney St. S40 22 A4
Sylvan Clo. S41 22 D6
Tap La. S40 22 B4
Tapton La. S41 22 D4
Tapton Ter. S41 22 D3
Tapton View Rd. S41 22 B2
Tennyson Av. S40 22 C4
The Bungalows. S40 22 A5
The Glade. S40 22 A4
*The Pavements,
  Low Pavement. S40 22 C4
*The Shambles,
  High St. S40 22 C4
*Theatre La,
  Tapton La. S41 22 D4
*Tontine Rd, New
  Beetwell St. S40 22 C4
Trinity Clo. S41 22 C3
*Trinity Ct,
  Newbold Rd. S41 22 A1

Tunstall Grn. S40 22 A6
Tunstall Way. S40 22 A6
Vernon Rd. S40 22 A4
Vicar La. S40 22 C4
Victoria St. S41 22 C3
Walgrove Av. S40 22 A5
Walgrove Rd. S40 22 A5
Walton Cres. S40 22 A6
Walton Dri. S40 22 A6
*Walton Dri Ct,
  Walton Dri. S40 22 A6
Walton Walk. S40 22 B5
Wardlow Clo. S40 22 B6
Webster Ct. S40 22 A2
Welfare Av. S40 22 A4
Welshpool Pl. S40 22 A4
Welshpool Yard. S40 22 A5
West Bars. S40 22 B4
West St. S40 22 B3
West View Rd. S41 22 A1
Wharf La. S41 22 D4
Wheatbridge Rd. S40 22 B4
Whitebank Clo. S41 22 D6
Whitworth Rd. S41 22 C1
William St. S41 22 C1

CLAY CROSS

Amber Pl. S45 23 A1
Appian Way. S45 23 B3
Ashbourne Av. S45 23 E4
Back Croft. S45 23 E4
Baileys Sq. S45 23 C2
Beech Way. S45 23 E3
Bennison Gdns. S45 23 D3
Beresford Clo. S45 23 D4
Bertrand Av. S45 23 D2
Bestwood Dri. S45 23 D2
Bestwood Park. S45 23 D2
Bevan Rd. S45 23 D3
Biggin Clo. S45 23 D2
Brackendale Av. S45 23 E4
Bradwell Gro. S45 23 D4
Brassington St. S45 23 D1
Bridge St. S45 23 C2
Broadleys. S45 23 C3
Brockway Clo. S45 23 E3
Brook St. S45 23 A1
Cannell Clo. S45 23 C2
Carlton Clo. S45 23 D3
Cavell Dri. S45 23 E3
Cemetery Rd. S45 23 D3
Chavery Rd. S45 23 E2
Church Av. S45 23 E3
Church La. S42 23 F1
Church Mdws. S42 23 F1
Clay La. S45 23 B3
Colliers Way. S45 23 C2
Commonpiece Rd. S45 23 B3
Coniston Rd. S45 23 B3
Coral Way. S45 23 D1
Coupe La. S45 23 A1
Cowsell Dri. S45 23 E4
Cromford Rd. S45 23 A1
Cross St. S45 23 C3
Denham St. S45 23 D3
Derby Rd. S42 23 C1
Derwent Pl. S45 23 B1
Dunshill Walk. S45 23 E2
Dunvegan Av. S45 23 E4
East St. S45 23 D2
Egstow Pl. S45 23 D2
Egstow St. S45 23 D1
Eldon St. S45 23 C2
Elm Gro. S45 23 D2
Eyre St. S45 23 C2
Flaxpiece Rd. S45 23 D3
Florence Rd. S45 23 E1
Furnace Hill. S45 23 D1
Garrett Grn. S45 23 E3
Garrett La. S45 23 E3
Gentshill Av. S45 23 E3
George Percival Pl.
  S45 23 B1
Grasmere Av. S45 23 B1
Grundy Rd. S45 23 C3
Guildford Clo. S45 23 E2
Guildford La. S45 23 E3
Hall Ter. S45 23 D2
Handley La. S45 23 A4
Harport Dri. S45 23 E4
High Hazles Clo. S45 23 E1

*High Hazles Walk,
  High Hazles Clo. S45 23 E1
High St. S45 23 C2
Hill St. S45 23 C2
Holmgate Rd. S45 23 A2
Jackson Rd. S45 23 E2
John St. S45 23 D1
Kenmere Clo. S45 23 D3
Kenning St. S45 23 D3
King St. S45 23 C3
Lathkill Gro. S45 23 D4
Lime Tree Gro. S45 23 E3
Linacre Av. S45 23 E4
Linden Av. S45 23 D3
Linden Ct. S45 23 D3
Lower Mantle Clo. S45 23 D1
Lynam Clo. S45 23 E3
Market St. S45 23 C2
Markham Rise. S45 23 C2
Meadow Rd. S45 23 A1
Middle La. S45 23 E3
Mill La,
  Clay Cross. S45 23 C4
Mill La,
  Henmoor. S45 23 A2
Morton Av. S45 23 C2
Nethercroft La. S45 23 E3
Newmarket La. S45 23 A3
Nightingale La. S45 23 C3
North St. S45 23 B1
Oakdale Clo. S45 23 D2
Ox Clo. S45 23 D2
Pankhurst Pl. S45 23 C3
Park Row. S45 23 D2
Parkhouse Clo. S45 23 C2
Penistone Gdns. S45 23 E4
Penncroft Dri. S45 23 D3
Penncroft La. S45 23 D3
Penncroft St. S45 23 E3
Peters Av. S45 23 C2
Pilsley Rd. S45 23 E3
Pine View. S45 23 E3
Piper Av. S45 23 E1
Pit La. S45 23 F2
Princess Pl. S45 23 C3
Pringvale Clo. S45 23 E4
Queen St. S45 23 C3
Riber Cres. S42 23 B1
Rock Cres. S45 23 A1
Rose Ct. S45 23 A1
Rydal Way. S45 23 B3
Rye Cres. S45 23 D3
Rykneld Ct. S45 23 E2
Shafton Clo. S45 23 E2
Shafton Walk. S45 23 E2
Slater St. S45 23 D3
Smithy Av. S45 23 C2
Springvale Clo. S45 23 E4
Springvale Rd. S45 23 D3
Stephenson Pl. S45 23 B2
Stollard St. S45 23 D2
Stoneholes Dri. S45 23 E4
Stretton Rd. S45 23 C3
Thanet St. S45 23 C3
The Crescent. S45 23 C3
The Fairways. S45 23 E3
The Square. S45 23 E3
Tranmere Av. S45 23 D2
Trelawney Rd. S45 23 D2
Upper Croft. S45 23 E3
Upper Mantle Clo. S45 23 D1
Valley Rd. S45 23 A1
Victoria St. S45 23 C3
Watercress La. S45 23 D4
Waterloo St. S45 23 D2
Wensley Rd. S42 23 F1
West St. S45 23 B1
Wheatcroft Clo. S45 23 D3
Wilson Clo. S45 23 E3
Windermere Rd. S45 23 B1
Winster Clo. S42 23 B1
Wolfscote Clo. S45 23 D4
Woodside Pl. S45 23 B1
Woodthorpe Av. S45 23 B1

CLOWNE

Ash Tree Rd. S43 29 B6
Ashlea Grn. S43 29 D4
Ashlea Walk. S43 29 D4
Barlborough Rd. S43 29 A4
Barton St. S43 29 C5

Beech Tree Dri. S43 29 C6
Bentinck Dri. S43 29 D5
Border Clo. S43 29 C6
Border Rd. S43 29 C6
Boughton La. S43 29 A4
Bramlyn Clo. S43 29 A4
Bramlyn Ct. S43 29 A4
Bricky Clo. S43 29 C4
Brook La. S43 29 C4
Brookbank Rd. S43 29 C4
Brookhill. S43 29 B4
Cavendish Dri. S43 29 D5
Chapel Clo. S43 29 C5
Chatsworth Av. S43 29 C5
Cherry Tree Clo. S43 29 C6
Chestnut Dri. S43 29 A5
Church Clo. S43 29 C5
Church La. S43 29 C5
Church St. S43 29 B5
Church Vw. S43 29 B5
Cliff Hill. S43 29 A5
Clumber Clo. S43 29 C4
Clune St. S43 29 D4
College Vw. S43 29 B5
Court Vw. S43 29 B6
Craggs Dri. S43 29 B6
Creswell Rd. S43 29 B4
Cricket Vw. S43 29 B5
Crown St. S43 29 B5
Damsbrook Dri. S43 29 B6
Devonshire Way. S43 29 C5
Duke St. S43 29 D5
Dukeries Ct. S43 29 C6
East St. S43 29 D4
Elmton Clo. S43 29 C6
Field Vw. S43 29 C6
Gapsick La. S43 29 C5
Gray St. S43 29 C5
Haddon Av. S43 29 D5
Hardwick Clo. S43 29 D5
Harlesthorpe Av. S43 29 C4
Harlesthorpe La. S43 29 B4
Hartington Ct. S43 29 D5
Hawthorn Clo. S43 29 A4
Heritage Dri. S43 29 A4
Hickinwood Cres. S43 29 C4
Hickinwood La. S43 29 C4
High Leys Rd. S43 29 B6
High St. S43 29 A5
Hollin Hill. S43 29 D6
Hutchings Cres. S43 29 A4
Jago Av. S43 29 D4
John St. S43 29 A6
Jubilee Cres. S43 29 D4
King St. S43 29 B6
Kings Clo. S43 29 C6
Lea Vw. S43 29 A4
Manor Ct. S43 29 C6
Mansfield Rd. S43 29 B6
Markland Av. S43 29 D4
Markland Clo. S43 29 D4
Markland La. S43 29 D6
Mastin Av. S43 29 A4
Meadow Vw. S43 29 C5
Mill Clo. S43 29 B5
Mill St. S43 29 B5
Mitchell St. S43 29 B5
Monnies End. S43 29 A4
Mount Pleasant Rd.
  S43 29 A6
Neale St. S43 29 C5
New Barlborough Clo.
  S43 29 A4
North Rd. S43 29 B4
Northfields. S43 29 C6
Oak Tree Rd. S43 29 B6
Offridge Clo. S43 29 B6
Orchard Clo. S43 29 B6
Park Vw. S43 29 C4
Parkfields. S43 29 C5
Pavilion Clo. S43 29 B6
Peak Vw. S43 29 A4
Pitch Clo. S43 29 B6
Portland St. S43 29 A6
Prospect Cotts. S43 29 B4
Ramper Av. S43 29 A4
Recreation Clo. S43 29 B4
Rectory Rd. S43 29 B5
Regent St. S43 29 A5
Rhodes Cotts. S43 29 C6
Ridgeway. S43 29 C6
Ridgeway West. S43 29 B6
Ringer La. S43 29 B5
Ringer Way. S43 29 B5

DERBY CITY CENTRE

DRAYCOTT

DRONFIELD

Firthwood Clo. S18 27 H2
Firthwood Rd. S18 27 H2
Fletcher Av. S18 27 E4
Ford Clo. S18 26 D4
Forresters La. S18 27 G1
Forth Av. S18 26 B3
Gainsborough Rd. S18 26 C4
Gardom Clo. S18 26 B4
Garth Way. S18 26 D4
Garth Way Clo. S18 26 D4
Gelderd Pl. S18 27 E5
Gledhill Clo. S18 27 E4
Gomersal La. S18 27 E4
Gorsey Brigg. S18 26 B4
Gosforth Clo. S18 26 D4
Gosforth Cres. S18 26 D4
Gosforth Dri. S18 26 B4
Gosforth Grn. S18 26 D4
Gosforth La. S18 26 D4
Grange Av. S18 26 C4
Grasmere Rd. S18 26 C4
Great Croft. S18 26 B3
Green Cross. S18 27 F3
Green La. S18 27 F2
Green Lea. S18 26 A3
Greenacres Clo. S18 27 G6
*Greendale Ct,
  Stonelow Rd. S18 27 F3
Grisdale Walk. S18 26 C4
Haddon Clo. S18 27 F3
Halfacre La. S18 27 H5
Hall Clo. S18 26 A3
Hallam Ct. S18 27 E5
Hallowes Ct. S18 27 F4
Hallowes Dri. S18 27 F5
Hallowes La. S18 27 F4
Hallowes Rise. S18 27 G5
Hanbury Clo. S18 26 D4
Hardwick Clo. S18 27 F3
Harington Rd. S18 27 F3
Hatton Clo. S18 26 B5
Hawkshead Av. S18 26 C4
Hawthorne Av. S18 27 E2
Hayfield Clo. S18 26 B4
Hazel Clo. S18 27 F5
Hazel Ct. S18 27 F5
Hazelwood Clo. S18 26 A4
Heatherfield Clo. S18 26 B4
Heaton Clo. S18 26 B4
High St. S18 27 E3
Highfields Cres. S18 27 E5
Highfields Rd. S18 27 E5
Highgate Dri. S18 27 G6
Highgate La. S18 27 F6
Hillside Av. S18 27 E5
Hilltop Rd. S18 27 E5
Hilltop Way. S18 27 E6
Hogarth Rise. S18 26 D5
Holbein Clo. S18 26 D5
Holborn Av. S18 27 E3
Hollies Clo. S18 27 F5
Hollins Spring Av. S18 27 E5
Hollins Spring Rd. S18 27 E5
Holm Clo. S18 26 B3
Holmesdale. S18 27 F2
Holmesdale Rd. S18 27 F2
Holmley Bank. S18 27 E2
Holmley La. S18 27 E2
Ingleby Clo. S18 26 B4
Ivanbrook Clo. S18 26 B4
Kendal Dri. S18 26 C4
Kentmere Clo. S18 26 C4
Keswick Clo. S18 26 C4
Kilburn Rd. S18 26 A4
Kiln Hill. S18 27 G2
Kipling Clo. S18 27 G5
Landseer Clo. S18 26 C4
Langdale Dri. S18 27 G2
Lea Rd. S18 27 E4
Leabrook Rd. S18 26 A4
Linden Av. S18 27 F2
Lindisfarne Rd. S18 27 F5
Links Rd. S18 27 F5
Longacre Rd. S18 27 E6
Longcroft Av. S18 26 A3
Longcroft Cres. S18 26 A3
Longcroft Rd. S18 26 A3
Lorne Clo. S18 26 B3
Lowry Dri. S18 26 D4
Lundy Rd. S18 26 B4
Lynwood Clo. S18 26 B4
Machin Ct. S18 27 E3
Manor Cres. S18 26 D4
Mapperley Rd. S18 26 A4

Marsh Av. S18 27 E2
Marston Clo. S18 26 B5
Meadow Clo. S18 27 G1
Melbourne Av. S18 26 A4
Mill La. S18 27 F4
Millstone Clo. S18 26 B3
Montrose Pl. S18 26 B3
Moonpenny Way. S18 27 E4
Moorgate Cres. S18 27 F5
Moray Pl. S18 26 B3
Morley Clo. S18 26 A4
Nairn Dri. S18 26 B4
Netherdene Rd. S18 27 E4
Netherfields Cres. S18 27 E5
Newstead Clo. S18 26 A4
Norbury Clo. S18 26 B4
Northern Common.
  S18 26 A3
Oakdell. S18 27 G2
Oakhill Rd. S18 27 G3
Orchard Sq. S18 26 B3
Ormesby Clo. S18 26 A4
Oxclose Dri. S18 26 A4
Oxclose La. S18 26 A4
Paddock Way. S18 27 F2
Palmer Cres. S18 27 F4
Park Av. S18 27 F3
Peel Gdns. S18 27 G3
Pembroke Rd. S18 27 E5
Pentland Rd. S18 26 B4
Pighills La. S18 27 F1
Poplar Clo. S18 27 F6
Potterdale Clo. S18 26 C4
Princess Rd. S18 27 E3
Prospect Rd. S18 27 G2
Quoit Grn. S18 27 F4
*Radbourne Common,
  Pentland Rd. S18 26 B4
Ravensdale Rd. S18 26 B4
Rembrandt Gdns. S18 26 C4
Repton Pl. S18 26 A4
Reynolds Clo. S18 26 D4
Ridgeway. S18 27 G2
*Rockingham Clo,
  Wentworth Rd. S18 26 A4
Romney Dri. S18 26 C4
Roston Clo. S18 26 B4
Rothay Clo. S18 26 C4
*Rowlins Ct,
  Birches Fold. S18 27 G1
Rubens Clo. S18 26 D4
Rydal Clo. S18 26 C4
Salisbury Av. S18 27 E5
Salisbury Rd. S18 27 F5
*Scarsdale Clo,
  Scarsdale Rd. S18 27 E4
Scarsdale Clo. S18 27 E5
*Scarsdale Cross,
  Scarsdale Rd. S18 27 E4
School La. S18 27 E4
Shakespeare Cres. S18 27 G5
Shaw St. S18 27 G1
Sheards Clo. S18 26 D3
Sheards Dri. S18 26 C4
Sheards Way. S18 26 D4
Sheffield Rd. S18 26 D2
Shelley Dri. S18 27 G6
*Sherwood Pl,
  Sherwood Rd. S18 26 B4
Sherwood Rd. S18 26 B4
Shetland Rd. S18 27 F5
Shireoaks Rd. S18 27 G3
Smithy Croft. S18 26 B3
Snape Hill. S18 27 E3
Snape Hill La. S18 27 E3
Snapehill Clo. S18 27 E2
Snapehill Cres. S18 27 E2
Snapehill Dri. S18 27 E2
Snelston Clo. S18 26 B4
Soaper La. S18 27 E3
Soloway Rise. S18 26 B3
Southcote Dri. S18 26 B4
Southfield Dri. S18 27 G5
Southfield Mnt. S18 27 G5
Southwood Av. S18 27 E6
Stafford Clo. S18 26 A3
Stanford Rd. S18 26 B4
Stone Clo. S18 27 G2
Stone Rd. S18 27 G1
Stonelow Cres. S18 27 G3
Stonelow Rd. S18 27 F3
Stubley Clo. S18 26 C2
Stubley Croft. S18 26 B3

Stubley Dri. S18 26 C3
Stubley Hollow. S18 26 C2
Stubley La. S18 26 C3
Stubley Pl. S18 26 D3
Summerfield Rd. S18 27 F2
Summerwood La. S18 26 D2
Summerwood Pl. S18 26 D3
Sycamore Av. S18 27 E2
Tay Clo. S18 26 B3
The Avenue. S18 27 F3
The Knoll. S18 27 G2
The Lawn. S18 27 F3
Thirlmere Dri. S18 27 E3
Thornton Rd. S18 26 B4
Thorpe Av. S18 27 F1
Trent Gro. S18 27 F2
*Turner Clo,
  Coniston Rd. S18 26 C4
Ullswater Clo. S18 26 C3
Ullswater Dri. S18 26 C3
Ullswater Park. S18 26 C4
Ullswater Pl. S18 26 C4
Unstone Dronfield
  By-Pass. S18 26 D3
Unstone Hill. S18 27 H5
Upper School La. S18 27 E4
Vale Clo. S18 27 E4
Victoria St. S18 26 D3
Walton Clo. S18 26 A3
Warren Rise. S18 27 G2
Welbeck Clo. S18 26 B3
Wentworth Rd. S18 26 A4
West St. S18 26 D3
Westbank Clo. S18 27 F1
*Westbank Ct,
  Westbank Clo. S18 27 F1
Westfield Rd. S18 27 E5
Wilson Rd. S18 27 G1
Wilson St. S18 27 F5
Windermere Av. S18 26 C4
Windsor Dri. S18 26 A4
Wingfield Clo. S18 26 A4
Wordsworth Pl. S18 27 G6
Wreakes La. S18 26 D2

DUFFIELD

Avenue Rd. DE56 25 B2
Breedon Av. DE56 25 B4
Broadway. DE56 25 B4
Broom Clo. DE56 25 B4
*Canterbury Clo, New
  Zealand La. DE56 25 B4
Castle Hill. DE56 25 C2
Castle Orchard. DE56 25 C2
Cavendish Clo. DE56 25 B4
Chadfield Rd. DE56 25 C1
Champion Hill. DE56 25 C3
Chapel St. DE56 25 C3
Chestnut Clo. DE56 25 C5
Chevin Bank. DE56 25 B1
Chevin Rd. DE56 25 B2
Chevin Vale. DE56 25 C1
Church Walk. DE56 25 D5
Crown St. DE56 25 C3
Cumberhills Rd. DE56 25 A5
Curzon St. DE56 25 C3
Curzon La. DE56 25 B4
*De Ferrers Ct,
  Tamworth St. DE56 25 C3
Derby Rd. DE56 25 C1
Devonshire Dri. DE56 25 B4
Donald Hawley Way.
  DE56 25 D4
Duck Island. DE56 25 C3
Eaton Ct. DE56 25 C5
Ecclesbourne Av.
  DE56 25 C4
Ecclesbourne Clo.
  DE56 25 C4
Eyes Ct. DE56 25 C4
Fairlawns. DE56 25 A4
Ferrers Cres. DE56 25 A4
Fisher La. DE56 25 C3
Gilbert St. DE56 25 C5
Golf La. DE56 25 C1
Granville Clo. DE56 25 C4
Haley Croft. DE56 25 D6
Hall Farm Rd. DE56 25 B4
Hazel Gro. DE56 25 B4
Hazeldene Clo. DE56 25 B1
Hazelwood Rd. DE56 25 A1

Hill Vw. DE56 25 B4
Holloway Rd. DE56 25 B3
King St. DE56 25 C2
Lime Av. DE56 25 C2
Lodge Clo. DE56 25 C4
Makeney Rd. DE56 25 D5
Marsden Clo. DE56 25 C4
Mayfair Ct. DE56 25 C2
Meadow Vale. DE56 25 A3
Meadows Croft. DE56 25 B4
Melbourne Dri. DE56 25 C4
Milford Rd. DE56 25 C3
Nether Clo. DE56 25 B1
New Zealand La. DE56 25 B4
Oak Clo. DE56 25 C4
Old Hall Av. DE56 25 B4
Old Mill Clo. DE56 25 B3
Park Rd. DE56 25 B4
Philips Croft. DE56 25 C2
Richmond Dri. DE56 25 B1
St Alkmunds Clo.
  DE56 25 C2
St Alkmunds Way.
  DE56 25 C2
St Ronans Av. DE56 25 C4
Scarsdale Rd. DE56 25 B4
Snake La. DE56 25 B3
Springfield Dri. DE56 25 B4
Station App. DE56 25 C3
Station Rd. DE56 25 C3
Stiles Walk. DE56 25 D3
*Tamworth Rise,
  Tamworth St. DE56 25 C3
Tamworth St. DE56 25 C3
Tamworth Ter. DE56 25 C3
The Pastures. DE56 25 C3
Town St. DE56 25 C3
Vicarage La. DE56 25 C2
Village Ct. DE56 25 C4
Wiltra Gro. DE56 25 D4
Wirksworth Rd. DE56 25 A3

ECKINGTON

Aintree Av. S31 29 A2
Albert St. S31 29 A3
Ash Cres. S31 29 A3
Ashland Rd. S31 29 D1
Ashleigh Ct. S31 29 A2
Ashmore Av. S31 29 A2
Aspen Rd. S31 29 A3
Back La. S31 29 A1
Bakehouse La. S31 29 C2
Barratt Rd. S31 29 C2
Beech Cres. S31 29 B2
Berry Av. S31 29 B2
Billam St. S31 29 B2
Bolehill La. S31 29 A3
Broomhill Clo. S31 29 A1
Camms Clo. S31 29 C1
Cary Rd. S31 29 A2
Castle Hill. S31 29 C1
Castle Hill Clo. S31 29 C1
Castle Vw. S31 29 C1
Cedar Clo. S31 29 A3
Chesterfield Rd. S31 29 A3
Chestnut Av. S31 29 A3
Church St. S31 29 D1
Curlew Av. S31 29 A2
Darcy Rd. S31 29 B2
Dronfield Rd. S31 29 A2
Ducksett La. S31 29 C2
East View Av. S31 29 B3
Edward St. S31 29 C2
Elm Rd. S31 29 B3
Fanshaw Av. S31 29 B2
Fanshaw Clo. S31 29 B3
Fanshaw Dri. S31 29 B3
Fanshaw Rd. S31 29 B2
Fanshaw Way. S31 29 B2
Fenton St. S31 29 A3
Fern Clo. S31 29 A2
Fern Way. S31 29 A2
Fernbank Dri. S31 29 B3
Fir Rd. S31 29 B3
Gosber Rd. S31 29 C2
Gosber St. S31 29 C2
Green Chase. S31 29 B1
Greenfields. S31 29 B1
Greenhall Rd. S31 29 B1
Hardie St. S31 29 C2
Hawks Way. S31 29 A2

Hawthorne Rd. S31 29 A3
Hayfield Vw. S31 29 B1
Hazel Rd. S31 29 B3
Henry St. S31 29 C2
High St. S31 29 B2
Highwood Pl. S31 29 B2
Hornthorpe Rd. S31 29 A3
Hunsdon Rd. S31 29 B2
Idas Rd. S31 29 C1
John St. S31 29 C2
Joseph St. S31 29 C2
Kestrel Clo. S31 29 A2
Kings Mews. S31 29 D1
Lady Idas Dri. S31 29 A1
Ladybank Vw. S31 29 C1
Lansbury Rd. S31 29 C2
Larch Rd. S31 29 A3
Laurel Clo. S31 29 B3
Lime Rd. S31 29 A3
Littlemoor. S31 29 D1
Market St. S31 29 C1
Marsh View. S31 29 C1
Martin Ct. S31 29 B1
Martin Rise. S31 29 B1
Mary St. S31 29 C2
Mill Rd. S31 29 D1
Moss Beck Ct. S31 29 B2
*Moss Rise Pl,
  West St. S31 29 B2
Mulberry Rd. S31 29 A3
North Gate. S31 29 C1
Osmund Rd. S31 29 A2
Park Hill. S31 29 D2
Partridge Clo. S31 29 A2
Pasture Gro. S31 29 D2
Penny Engine La. S31 29 D1
Peveril Rd. S31 29 D1
Pinfold St. S31 29 C1
Pipeyard La. S31 29 B2
Pitt St. S31 29 B3
Poplar Rd. S31 29 B3
Queen St. S31 29 D1
Randall St. S31 29 A3
Ravencar Rd. S31 29 A2
Rectory Clo. S31 29 D1
Rotherham Rd. S31 29 D1
Rotherside Rd. S31 29 D1
Rowan Rd. S31 29 B3
Royale Clo. S31 29 B3
Sandown Clo. S31 29 A2
School St. S31 29 C2
Setcup La. S31 29 B3
Sitwell St. S31 29 C2
Southgate. S31 29 C2
Southgate Clo. S31 29 D2
Springfield Clo. S31 29 B1
Staniforth Av. S31 29 A2
Station Rd. S31 29 D2
Staveley Clo. S31 29 D3
Stead St. S31 29 C1
The Bungalows. S31 29 B2
Valley View Clo. S31 29 B3
Watermeade. S31 29 A2
West End View. S31 29 B2
West St. S31 29 B2
William St. S31 29 C2
Wulfric Rd. S31 29 B2

GLOSSOP

Acre Ct. SK13 30 D4
Acre Rd. SK13 30 C4
Appleton Dri. SK13 30 F3
Arden Clo. SK13 30 A4
Arundel Grange. SK13 30 A3
Ashbourne Ct. SK13 30 F3
Ashes La. SK13 30 B2
Ashleigh Av. SK13 30 C1
Ashton Gdns. SK13 30 C4
Ashton St. SK13 30 C4
Ashwood. SK13 30 A4
Bank St. SK13 30 D3
Barn Clo. SK13 30 A3
Beech Av. SK13 30 A3
Bernard St. SK13 30 C2
Bexley Clo. SK13 30 C1
Birch Grn. SK13 30 E3
Birchside Av. SK13 30 B2
Blackshaw Rd. SK13 30 E1
*Booth Ct,
  Norfolk St. SK13 30 D3
Bowden Rd. SK13 30 D1

Bowland Rd. SK13 30 A3
Bracken Way. SK13 30 F4
Brendon Clo. SK13 30 B3
Brights Ter. SK13 30 E4
Brook Meadow. SK13 30 E2
Brook St. SK13 30 C3
Burwell Clo. SK13 30 A3
Bute St. SK13 30 E1
Castle St. SK13 30 E1
Cedar Clo. SK13 30 C1
Chadwick St. SK13 30 B3
Chapel St. SK13 30 C3
Charles La. SK13 30 F1
Charles St. SK13 30 D2
Charlestown Rd. SK13 30 C4
Church St. SK13 30 D1
Church St Sth. SK13 30 E1
Church Walk. SK13 30 E1
Cliffe Rd. SK13 30 D4
Collier St. SK13 30 D3
Cooper St. SK13 30 B3
Corn St. SK13 30 E2
Cotswold Clo. SK13 30 A4
Cowbrook Av. SK13 30 F2
Croft Manor. SK13 30 E3
Cross Cliffe. SK13 30 E3
Cross Rise. SK13 30 E3
Cross St. SK13 30 C3
Crosslands Clo. SK13 30 D3
Derby St. SK13 30 D3
Derwent Clo. SK13 30 F3
Dingle Clo. SK13 30 A3
Dinting La. SK13 30 A2
Dinting Rd. SK13 30 A1
Dinting Vale. SK13 30 A2
Dovedale Ct. SK13 30 F3
Drovers Walk. SK13 30 D2
Duke St. SK13 30 C3
*Dunne La,
Church St. SK13 30 E1
Ebenezer St. SK13 30 D4
Edward St. SK13 30 C2
Ellison St. SK13 30 D2
Elm Gro. SK13 30 C1
Fernhill Clo. SK13 30 D1
Fitzalan St. SK13 30 D2
Freetown. SK13 30 C4
Fresh Ct. SK13 30 A4
Furness Clo. SK13 30 F3
George St. SK13 30 C3
Gladstone St. SK13 30 D3
Glenbrook Hill. SK13 30 C1
Glossop Brook Rd.
SK13 30 B2
Gloucester Way. SK13 30 F3
Gorse Way. SK13 30 F4
Green Bank. SK13 30 A4
Green La. SK13 30 A4
Hadfield Pl. SK13 30 C3
*Hadfield Sq,
Victoria St. SK13 30 C3
Hadfield St. SK13 30 C3
Hague St. SK13 30 D4
Hall Meadow Rd. SK13 30 D1
*Halls Ct,
Chapel St. SK13 30 C3
Hampshire Clo. SK13 30 F3
Hathersage Dri. SK13 30 F4
Hawkshead Rd. SK13 30 E1
Haywards Clo. SK13 30 C1
Heath Rd. SK13 30 C1
Heather Bank Clo.
SK13 30 A4
Hebden Dri. SK13 30 F3
Henry St. SK13 30 D2
High La. SK13 30 A4
High St East. SK13 30 D3
High St West. SK13 30 A2
Highbank Rd. SK13 30 F4
Higher Dinting. SK13 30 B2
Highfield Rd. SK13 30 D3
Highview. SK13 30 A4
Highwood Clo. SK13 30 B4
Hilltop Rd. SK13 30 B1
Hillwood Dri. SK13 30 F3
Hollin Cross La. SK13 30 C3
Hope St. SK13 30 E1
Howard Clo. SK13 30 C1
Howard Pl. SK13 30 B3
Howard St. SK13 30 C2
Hugh St. SK13 30 B3
Hunters La. SK13 30 A3
Hurstbrook Clo. SK13 30 F3
Jackson St. SK13 30 C4
James St. SK13 30 C3
John St. SK13 30 C3
Jordan St. SK13 30 E2
*Junction Ct,
High St. SK13 30 B2
Kent Rd. SK13 30 D2
Kershaw St. SK13 30 D4
Kinder Clo. SK13 30 B3
King Charles Ct. SK13 30 D4
King Edward Av. SK13 30 D2
King St. SK13 30 D3
Kingsmoor Fields.
SK13 30 D1
Kingsmoor Rd. SK13 30 D1
Langley Dri. SK13 30 F4
Larch Way. SK13 30 F3
Lee Mnt. SK13 30 C4
Leicester Clo. SK13 30 F3
Leicester Dri. SK13 30 F4
Linacre Way. SK13 30 F4
Lincoln Way. SK13 30 F3
Longclough Dri. SK13 30 B3
Longmoor Rd. SK13 30 A4
Lord St. SK13 30 D2
Lower Bank. SK13 30 D3
Lyne Av. SK13 30 A3
Lynne Clo. SK13 30 F3
Manor Park Rd. SK13 30 E2
Manor Park Vw. SK13 30 E2
Manor St. SK13 30 D3
Market St. SK13 30 C3
Meadow Rise. SK13 30 A4
Melanie Clo. SK13 30 A4
Mill St. SK13 30 D3
Millersdale Ct. SK13 30 F3
Milltown. SK13 30 D3
Morley St. SK13 30 E3
Mount St. SK13 30 C3
Norfolk Sq. SK13 30 D3
Norfolk St. SK13 30 D3
North Rd. SK13 30 C1
Nursery Clo. SK13 30 C3
Oak St. SK13 30 C2
Off Hope St. SK13 30 F1
Old Hall Clo. SK13 30 D2
Old La. SK13 30 A4
Padfield Gate. SK13 30 D4
Park Clo. SK13 30 D2
Park Cres. SK13 30 C1
Park Dean. SK13 30 C1
Park Ter. SK13 30 C3
Partington Ct. SK13 30 F3
Peaknaze Clo. SK13 30 B3
Pennine Rd. SK13 30 A3
Peveril Ct. SK13 30 F3
Phillip Howard Rd.
SK13 30 C3
Pikes La. SK13 30 B3
Primrose Cres SK13 30 B3
Primrose Hill. SK13 30 B3
Primrose La. SK13 30 A3
Princess St. SK13 30 C3
Pye Gro. SK13 30 F2
Pyegrove Rd. SK13 30 F2
Quarry Clo. SK13 30 D2
Queen St. SK13 30 B3
Queens Dri. SK13 30 F2
Railway St. SK13 30 C2
Ramsden Clo. SK13 30 D1
Regent St. SK13 30 D2
Riverbank Way. SK13 30 F4
Riverside Clo. SK13 30 D2
*Riverview Cotts,
Ashton Gdns. SK13 30 C4
Royle Av. SK13 30 D2
St Fauvel Rd. SK13 30 C2
St James Clo. SK13 30 C4
St Marys Rd. SK13 30 C3
Sandway. SK13 30 F4
School St. SK13 30 C3
Sefton St. SK13 30 C3
Shaw St. SK13 30 C3
Sheffield Rd. SK13 30 E2
Shepley St. SK13 30 E1
Shire Way. SK13 30 E1
Shirebrook Dri. SK13 30 E3
Shrewsbury St. SK13 30 C2
Shropshire Dri. SK13 30 F4
Silk St. SK13 30 E2
Simmondley Gro.
SK13 30 A3
Simmondley La. SK13 30 A3
Simmondley New Rd.
SK13 30 A4
Simons Clo. SK13 30 A4
Simons Walk. SK13 30 A4
Slant Clo. SK13 30 E3
Slatelands. SK13 30 B4
Slatelands Av. SK13 30 C3
Smedley Pl. SK13 30 E1
Smithy Clo. SK13 30 D2
Smithy Fold. SK13 30 D3
Southview Rd. SK13 30 F4
Spinney Clo. SK13 30 C2
Spire Hollin. SK13 30 C1
Spring Rise. SK13 30 A4
Spring St. SK13 30 B3
Stafford Clo. SK13 30 F3
Station St. SK13 30 D2
Storth Meadow Rd.
SK13 30 A4
Summers Pl. SK13 30 B3
Sumner St. SK13 30 C3
Sunlaws St. SK13 30 B3
Sunny Bank. SK13 30 B3
Surrey St. SK13 30 C2
Talbot Rd. SK13 30 C1
Talbot St. SK13 30 D2
Tarn Side. SK13 30 A4
Tenfoot Clo. SK13 30 B2
The Bank. SK13 30 D3
The Green. SK13 30 A4
The Oaks. SK13 30 B4
Thomas St. SK13 30 E2
Thorpe St. SK13 30 E1
Todd St. SK13 30 D4
Tredcroft St. SK13 30 C3
Turnlee Clo. SK13 30 C4
Turnlee Dri. SK13 30 C4
Turnlee Rd. SK13 30 C4
Union St. SK13 30 D3
Unity Walk. SK13 30 D4
Uplands Rd. SK13 30 D4
Victoria St. SK13 30 C3
Warwick Clo. SK13 30 F3
Water St. SK13 30 F1
Wellgate. SK13 30 E1
Werneth Rd. SK13 30 A3
Wesley St. SK13 30 E1
Whitfield Av. SK13 30 C4
Whitfield Cross. SK13 30 D4
Wilsons Ter. SK13 30 B3
Wiltshire Dri. SK13 30 F3
Wingfield Gro. SK13 30 F4
Winnats Clo. SK13 30 F3
Wood St. SK13 30 D4
Woodcock Gro. SK13 30 F2
Woodhead Rd. SK13 30 D1
Worcester Gro. SK13 30 F4
Wren Nest Rd. SK13 30 B2
Wren Nest Ter. SK13 30 C2
York St. SK13 30 E2
York Ter. SK13 30 C4
Yorkshire Way. SK13 30 F3

HEANOR

Abbott St. DE75 31 A4
Adams Clo. DE75 31 A6
Admiral Clo. DE75 31 A4
Aldercar By-Pass.
NG16 31 B1
Aldercar La. NG16 31 D1
Aldreds La. DE75 31 C4
Allandale Rd. DE75 31 A3
Amber Ct. DE75 31 A4
Amber Dri. NG16 31 D3
Andrews Dri. NG16 31 C2
Ardsley Clo. DE75 31 C3
Argyle St. NG16 31 D2
Ascote Clo. DE75 31 C4
Ashforth Av. DE75 31 C5
Ashmount Rd. NG16 31 D3
Avis Av. DE75 31 B6
Bailey Brook Cres.
NG16 31 C2
Bailey Brook Dri. NG16 31 C2
Bailey Brook Dri. DE75 31 A1
Bailey Brook Wk. NG16 31 C2
Baker Av. DE75 31 B6
Bassford Av. DE75 31 B3
Berle Av. DE75 31 A3
Bestwick Av. DE75 31 D4
Birchfield Park. DE75 31 B6
Bircum Shaw Rd.
DE75 31 A4
Brampton Av. DE75 31 C3
Breach Rd. DE75 31 C5
Broadway. DE75 31 A4
Brockhall Rise. DE75 31 C4
Brooklands Av. DE75 31 B3
Burns St. DE75 31 A3
Burnthouse Rd. DE75 31 A4
Burton St. DE75 31 A3
Buxton Av. DE75 31 B6
Buxton Grn. DE75 31 B6
Carlton Clo. DE75 31 C3
Carlyle Pl. DE75 31 A3
Carlyle St. DE75 31 A3
Castle Vw. NG16 31 C1
Chapel St. DE75 31 C5
Chestnut Rd. NG16 31 C2
Church St. DE75 31 B4
Claramount Rd. DE75 31 C4
Claxton St. DE75 31 A4
Claxton Ter. DE75 31 A4
Coppice Dri. DE75 31 B6
Corfield Av. DE75 31 B6
Cromford Clo. NG16 31 D1
Cromford Rd. NG16 31 C1
Daltons Clo. NG16 31 C1
*Darfield Dri, Wentworth
Croft. DE75 31 C3
Deepdale Ct. DE75 31 A5
Delves Rd. DE75 31 A5
Derby Rd. DE75 31 A4
Dodford Ct. DE75 31 C4
East Nelson St. DE75 31 A3
Eastview Ter. NG16 31 D2
Ebenezer St. NG16 31 D2
Edward St. NG16 31 D2
Ella Bank Rd. DE75 31 C4
Elmsfield Av. DE75 31 C3
England Cres. DE75 31 C3
Fairview. DE75 31 A4
Fall Rd. DE75 31 A3
Fast St. DE75 31 C5
Fletcher St. DE75 31 A3
Frederic Av. DE75 31 B6
Frost Av. NG16 31 C2
Garnett Av. DE75 31 B3
George St. NG16 31 D2
Gillott St. DE75 31 C5
Gladstone Av. DE75 31 B3
Gladstone St. DE75 31 B3
Godfrey St. DE75 31 A4
Godkin Dri. NG16 31 C1
Grace Cres. DE75 31 B4
Greenacre Av. DE75 31 C3
Greenfields. NG16 31 C1
Greggs Av. DE75 31 B3
Gregory Dri. NG16 31 C2
Hampden St. NG16 31 D2
Hands Rd. DE75 31 B4
Hardy Barn. DE75 31 C6
Harold Av. NG16 31 D2
Hassock Lane N. DE75 31 D6
Heanor Gate Rd. DE75 31 A5
Heyford Ct. DE75 31 C5
High St. DE75 31 A3
Hill Rd. DE75 31 A4
Hillside. NG16 31 C3
Hogbarn La.DE75 31 A1
Taylor La. DE75 31 A1
Holbrook St. DE75 31 C3
Holmes Clo. NG16 31 C2
Holmesfield Dri. DE75 31 B5
Homestead. NG16 31 D1
Horsley Cres. NG16 31 C2
Howitt St. DE75 31 B4
Huftons Ct. DE75 31 C6
Huftons Dri. DE75 31 C6
Hunt Av. DE75 31 B3
Ilkeston Rd. DE75 31 B4
INDUSTRIAL ESTATES:
Bailey Brook
Ind Est. NG16 31 D3
Joan Av. DE75 31 A3
John St. DE75 31 A3
Johns Pl. DE75 31 A4
Johnson Dri. DE75 31 B3
Julie Av. DE75 31 D4
Kew Cres. DE75 31 D5
Kings Way. DE75 31 A4
Kirkham Clo. DE75 31 A5
Lacy Fields Rd. DE75 31 C4
Lawn Clo. DE75 31 B3
Leafy La. DE75 31 C4
Lee La. DE75 31 D4
Lockton Av. DE75 31 A5
Longbridge La. DE75 31 A2
Loscoe Rd. DE75 31 A3
Lower Claramount Rd.
DE75 31 C4
Lower Dunstead Rd.
NG16 31 D3
Lower Gladstone St.
DE75 31 A3
Lower Maples. DE75 31 C6
Lowlands Lea. DE75 31 B3
Mansfield Rd. DE75 31 B4
Market Pl. DE75 31 B4
Market St. DE75 31 A4
Marshall St. DE75 31 C3
Mayfield Av. DE75 31 A4
Midland Rd. DE75 31 A3
Mill Rd. DE75 31 C5
Millbank. DE75 31 C5
Mitchell Av. NG16 31 C2
Mount Rd. DE75 31 C4
Mount St. DE75 31 A4
Mundy St. DE75 31 A4
Mundys Dri. DE75 31 B5
Nelson St. DE75 31 A3
Newham Clo. DE75 31 C4
Newlands Dri. DE75 31 B3
Nook End Rd. DE75 31 A4
North St. NG16 31 D2
Oak Av. NG16 31 D1
Oaklands Av. DE75 31 C3
Old Coppice Side.
DE75 31 A6
Oliver Clo. DE75 31 D3
Orchard Rise. DE75 31 B3
Orchard St. NG16 31 D3
Ormonde St. NG16 31 D1
Ormonde Ter. NG16 31 D1
Owers Av. DE75 31 B6
Park St. DE75 31 A3
Peach St. DE75 31 A5
Peel St. NG16 31 D3
Pine Av. NG16 31 C2
Plumptre Rd. NG16 31 D1
Prospect Rd. DE75 31 C5
Ray Av. DE75 31 A4
Ray St. DE75 31 A4
Red Lion Sq. DE75 31 A4
Regent St. NG16 31 D2
Ridgeway. DE75 31 C6
Roper Av. DE75 31 B5
Rosewood Cres. DE75 31 D3
St Laurence Clo. DE75 31 B4
Saxton Av. DE75 31 B3
Sedgewick St. NG16 31 D3
Slack La. DE75 31 A5
Smeeton St. DE75 31 D4
Smith Dri. NG16 31 C2
Spring La. DE75 31 A4
Stainsby Av. DE75 31 A5
Stamford St. DE75 31 A3
Starthe Bank. DE75 31 C4
Station Rd. NG16 31 D3
Stoddard Dri. DE75 31 B4
Sunningdale Av. DE75 31 B6
The Hamlet. DE75 31 A3
The Meadows. DE75 31 A4
Thistle Grn Clo. DE75 31 D4
Thompson St. NG16 31 D2
Thorpehill Dri. DE75 31 B6
Thorpes Rd. DE75 31 A4
Tudor Falls. DE75 31 A3
Turner Av. NG16 31 C2
Turton Clo. NG16 31 C2
Upper Barn Clo. DE75 31 B3
Upper Dunstead Rd.
NG16 31 D2
Upper Nelson St. DE75 31 A4
Upton Clo. DE75 31 C4
Watkinson St. DE75 31 A3
Watson Av. DE75 31 B3
Wentworth Croft. DE75 31 C3
West St. NG16 31 D3
Western Dri. DE75 31 B5
Westfield Av. DE75 31 B5
Weston St. DE75 31 C5
Whysall St. DE75 31 A4
Wilmot St. DE75 31 A5
Wood End Rd. DE75 31 A3

ILKESTON

Abbey St. DE7 32 C4
Abbot St. NG16 32 F2
Abbotsford Mews.
DE7 32 A3
Adam St. DE7 33 E8
Adams Ct. DE7 32 B3

Albany St. DE7 33 D7
Albert St. DE7 33 B6
Albion Centre. DE7 33 C5
Albion St. DE7 33 C5
Allendale. DE7 33 B7
Alvenor St. DE7 33 C5
Amilda Av. DE7 33 C6
Anchor Row. DE7 33 C6
Andrew Av. DE7 33 E6
Anson Walk. DE7 32 C3
Appleby Clo. DE7 33 C8
Archer St. DE7 32 B3
Ash St. DE7 32 B2
Ashdale Rd. DE7 33 D7
Ashford Pl. DE7 32 B1
Aston Ct. DE7 33 C5
Attewell Rd. NG16 32 C3
Audley Clo. DE7 32 A3
Avonlea Clo. DE7 33 E8
Awsworth By-Pass.
  NG16 32 E2
Awsworth
  Common Rd. DE7 32 D3
Awsworth La. NG16 32 F4
Awsworth Rd. DE7 32 C4
Back La. DE7 32 B4
Baker St. DE7 33 C5
Barber Clo. DE7 32 B4
Barclay Ct. DE7 32 A3
Barker Gate. DE7 32 C4
Barling Dri. DE7 32 A4
Barlow Dri Nth. NG16 32 E2
Barlow Dri Sth. NG16 32 E2
Bath St. DE7 33 C5
Beatty Walk. DE7 32 C3
Beauvale Dri. DE7 32 B1
Belfield St. DE7 32 C4
Belper St. DE7 33 C7
Belvoir Clo. DE7 33 A8
Benner Av. DE7 33 D8
Bennerley Av. DE7 32 C2
Berisford Dri. DE7 32 B1
Bethel St. DE7 33 C5
Birch Av. DE7 32 D7
Birchover Pl. DE7 32 B1
Birdcroft La. DE7 33 C8
Birkdale Dri. DE7 32 A4
Black Hills Dri. DE7 33 C7
Blackburn Pl. DE7 32 B3
Blake St. DE7 32 C5
Bloomsgrove Rd. DE7 32 C4
Boatmans Clo. DE7 32 C4
Bonners Rd. NG16 32 F2
Bonsall Pl. DE7 33 B5
Boscawen Ct. DE7 32 C3
Botany Dri. DE7 32 C1
Bowes Well Rd. DE7 32 B4
Breadsall Ct. DE7 32 C3
Bridge St. DE7 32 C2
Bright St. DE7 32 B3
Bristol Rd. DE7 33 B5
Broadway. DE7 32 B3
Brook Cotts. DE7 32 D3
Brooke St. DE7 33 E8
Broomhill Av. DE7 33 D8
Brussels Yd. DE7 33 C5
Buller St. DE7 33 D8
Burleigh St. DE7 33 C5
Burns St. DE7 33 B6
Burr La. DE7 33 C5
Butterton Clo. DE7 33 D7
Byron Cres. NG16 32 F2
Byron St. DE7 33 C5
Canal St. DE7 33 D5
Canon Clo. DE7 32 C1
Cantelupe Rd. DE7 33 C5
Caroline Ct. DE7 33 D7
Castleton Av. DE7 32 B1
Catherine Av. DE7 33 C8
Cavendish Rd. DE7 33 C8
Cedars Park. DE7 33 B6
*Chalons Clo,
  Chaucer St. DE7 33 C5
Chambers Av. DE7 33 E6
Chapel Ct. DE7 32 C2
Chapel St. DE7 33 C5
Charles Clo. DE7 33 E7
Charlotte St. DE7 32 B3
Charter Pk. DE7 33 B6
Chaucer St. DE7 33 C5
Chaucer St. DE7 33 C5
Cherrytree Clo. DE7 33 A8
Chesterman Clo. NG16 32 E2
Chichester Clo. DE7 33 D6

Church Dri. DE7 32 A2
Church La. NG16 32 F4
Church St. DE7 32 A2
Church Vw,
  Cotmanhay. DE7 32 B2
Church Vw,
  Little Hallam. DE7 33 B7
Clumber Ct. DE7 32 C1
Cook Dri. DE7 33 D8
Coppice Av. DE7 32 A2
Coronation Rd. DE7 32 D4
Coronation St. DE7 33 C6
Corporation Rd. DE7 33 D8
Cotmanhay Rd. DE7 32 C3
Cottage Clo. DE7 32 A3
Cranmer St. DE7 33 C5
Critchley St. DE7 32 B1
Croft Cres. NG16 32 F1
Cromwell Av. DE7 33 C8
Dale St. DE7 33 C7
Dale Vw. DE7 33 B7
Darley Sq. DE7 32 B1
Darwin Av. DE7 33 B6
Derby Rd. DE7 33 A7
Derby St. DE7 33 C6
Derbyshire Dri. DE7 33 B7
Derwent Av. DE7 32 B4
Devon St. DE7 33 D8
Devonshire Clo. DE7 32 B1
Digby St. DE7 33 D5
Donner Cres. DE7 32 B1
Doris Rd. DE7 33 D6
Dorterry Cres. DE7 33 D8
Douglas Av. DE7 32 B1
Dovedale Circle. DE7 32 A1
Draycott Ct. DE7 32 C3
Dronfield Pl. DE7 32 B1
Drummond Rd. DE7 33 B5
Duke St. DE7 32 C3
Dukes Pl. DE7 32 B2
Durham St. DE7 33 C5
Earl Pl. DE7 32 C4
East St. DE7 33 C6
Eaton Av. DE7 33 A8
Ebenezer St. DE7 32 C3
Edale Sq. DE7 32 B1
Eleanor Av. DE7 33 D8
Eley Clo. DE7 32 A4
Eliot St. DE7 33 A8
Elveden Dri. DE7 32 A2
Emsworth Clo. DE7 32 A3
Erewash Dri. DE7 33 D7
Erewash Sq. DE7 33 D7
Essex St. DE7 33 C5
Eyres Gdns. DE7 32 C4
Factory La. DE7 32 B4
Farfield Rd. DE7 33 D5
Farm Clo. DE7 33 D5
Field Rd. DE7 33 C7
First Av. DE7 33 C7
Fisher Ct. DE7 32 C2
Flamstead Rd. DE7 33 D5
Florence Ct. DE7 33 C5
French St. DE7 33 B7
Fullwood Av. DE7 33 B5
Fullwood St. DE7 33 B5
Furnace Rd. DE7 33 E8
Gallows Inn Clo. DE7 33 D8
Garden Av. DE7 33 C8
Gimson Clo. DE7 32 A3
Gin Close Way. NG16 32 F1
Gladstone St
  East. DE7 33 C6
Gladstone St
  West. DE7 33 C6
Glebe Cres. DE7 33 D7
Godfrey Dri. DE7 33 A8
Goole Av. DE7 33 A8
Gordon St. DE7 33 D5
Graham St. DE7 33 C6
Granby St. DE7 32 C4
Grangewood Av. DE7 33 C7
Grass St. DE7 32 B3
Green La. DE7 33 D6
Greenwood Av. DE7 33 D7
Gregory St. DE7 32 B3
Grenville Dri. DE7 33 B5
Gresley Rd. DE7 33 D5
Grove Ter. DE7 33 D5
Haddon Nurseries. DE7 32 B3
Haddon St. DE7 32 B3
Hadley St. DE7 33 D8
Hallam Ct. DE7 32 C6
Hallcroft Rd. DE7 33 C5

Hartington Pl. DE7 32 B1
Hassock La. DE7 32 A1
Havelock St. DE7 33 C7
Hawkins Ct. DE7 32 C2
Hawthorn Rise. NG16 32 E2
Hayes Clo. DE7 32 A4
Hayling Clo. DE7 32 A3
Heanor Rd. DE7 32 A1
Heathfield Av. DE7 33 D6
Hedges Clo. DE7 32 A4
Hemlock Way. DE7 33 A8
Henshaw Pl. DE7 32 B2
Hermitage Walk. DE7 33 C8
High Holborn Pl. DE7 32 B3
High St. DE7 33 C6
Highgate Dri. DE7 32 A3
Hobson Dri. DE7 33 B7
Holkham Clo. DE7 32 A3
Holme Clo. DE7 32 A4
Holmefield Cres. DE7 33 D6
Holywell Rd. DE7 32 A3
Honingham Rd. DE7 32 A3
Hope St. DE7 33 C6
Hopewell Walk. DE7 32 C2
Hornbeam Clo. DE7 33 E7
Horridge St. DE7 32 C2
Horsecroft Clo. DE7 32 A4
Houghton Av. DE7 32 A3
Huckleberry Rd. DE7 32 A4
Hungerhill Yard. DE7 33 D7
Ilam Sq. DE7 32 B1
Ilford Clo. DE7 32 A4
Ilkeston Rd. DE7 33 E8

INDUSTRIAL ESTATES:
Gallows Inn
  Ind Est. DE7 33 E7
Manners Ind Est. DE7 33 A5
Inglefield Rd. DE7 33 B5
Jackson Av. DE7 33 B5
Jervis Ct. DE7 32 C3
John Street. DE7 33 C5
Julian Ct. DE7 33 E8
Kedleston Dri. DE7 32 A3
Kenilworth Dri. DE7 33 A8
Kensington Gdns. DE7 33 D7
Kensington St. DE7 33 C7
Keppel Ct. DE7 32 C3
Kilburn Cres. DE7 32 A3
King George Av. DE7 33 B6
King St. DE7 33 C5
Kingsway. DE7 33 D8
Kirkby Av. DE7 33 C8
Kniveton Pk. DE7 33 A6
Ladywood Rd. DE7 33 A8
Lambton Clo. DE7 32 B3
Laneward Clo. DE7 32 A2
Langley Av. DE7 32 B1
Larklands Av. DE7 33 D6
Lathkill Av. DE7 32 B1
Lawrence Av. NG16 32 F2
Lee Cres. DE7 33 E6
Lilac Mews. DE7 32 A3
Lime St. DE7 33 C6
Lissett Av. DE7 33 D6
Litchen Clo. DE7 32 C3
Little Hallam Hill. DE7 33 B8
Little Hallam La. DE7 33 C8
Litton Clo. DE7 32 B3
Longfield Cres. DE7 33 C8
Longfield La. DE7 33 C8
Lord Haddon Rd. DE7 33 B5
Lower Bloomsgrove Rd.
  DE7 32 C4
Lower Chapel St. DE7 33 C5
Lower Granby St. DE7 32 C4
Lower Middleton St.
  DE7 33 D5
Lower Stanton Rd.
  DE7 33 C7
Lower Whitworth Rd.
  DE7 33 C8
Lynmouth Dri. DE7 32 A3
Main St. NG16 32 F1
Manners Av. DE7 33 A5
Manners Rd. DE7 33 B5
Manners St. DE7 33 B5
Manning Vw. DE7 32 C4
Manor Rd. DE7 33 B5
Manorfields Dri. DE7 33 A7
Margaret Av. DE7 33 C6
Market Pl. DE7 33 C6
Market St. DE7 33 C6
Marshall Way. DE7 33 A8
May St. DE7 32 B3

Meadow Rd. NG16 32 F1
Meadow St. DE7 33 C5
Middleton Rd. DE7 33 D8
Middleton St,
  Awsworth. NG16 32 F2
Middleton St,
  Ilkeston. DE7 32 D4
Milford Dri. DE7 32 A3
Mill La. NG16 33 F5
Mill St. DE7 33 C5
Millbank Clo. DE7 32 A3
Millers Dale. DE7 32 B1
Millfield Clo. DE7 32 A2
Millfield Rd. DE7 33 D6
Milton Av. DE7 32 B2
Milton Rd. DE7 32 C2
Milton St. DE7 32 C2
Monks Clo. DE7 33 D6
Monkton Clo. DE7 32 A3
Monsall Av. DE7 32 B1
Monyash Clo. DE7 32 B3
Morley Dri. DE7 32 A3
Moss Rd. DE7 33 B6
Mount Pleasant. DE7 32 C2
Mount St. DE7 33 C5
Mountbatten Ct. DE7 32 C3
Mundy St. DE7 32 C4
Muskham Av. DE7 32 C3
Nelper Cres. DE7 33 D8
Nelson St. DE7 32 C2
Nesfield Rd. DE7 33 B5
New Lawn Rd. DE7 33 B5
Newdigate St. DE7 33 D8
Newstead Rd Nth. DE7 32 A3
Newstead Rd Sth. DE7 32 A3
Newtons La. NG16 32 E3
Norman Cres. DE7 32 B3
Norman St. DE7 32 B3
North St. DE7 33 C5
Northfield Av. DE7 32 B4
Northgate St. DE7 33 C5
Nottingham Rd. DE7 33 C7
Nursery Hollow. DE7 33 C8
Oakham Way. DE7 32 B3
Oakwell Cres. DE7 33 B6
Oakwell Dri. DE7 33 B6
Ockbrook Ct. DE7 32 C3
Oliver Rd. DE7 33 A8
Orchard St. DE7 33 C7
Oxford St. DE7 33 C7
Park Av,
  Awsworth. NG16 32 E1
Park Av, Ilkeston. DE7 33 D6
Park Cres. DE7 33 D6
Park Dri. DE7 33 C7
Park Hill. NG16 32 E1
Park Rd. DE7 33 C6
Pavilion Rd. DE7 32 C1
Peacock Pl. DE7 32 B2
Pedley St. DE7 33 C7
Pelham Av. DE7 33 B5
Pelham St. DE7 33 B5
Pentridge Dri. DE7 32 A3
Percy St. DE7 33 C7
Peveril Dri. DE7 32 B4
Pimlico. DE7 33 B6
Poplar Way. DE7 33 A8
Portland Rd. DE7 32 C3
Potters La. DE7 33 D6
Potters Way. DE7 33 D6
Powtrill Pl. DE7 33 E7
Primrose Hill. DE7 32 C3
Primrose St. DE7 32 C3
Prince St. DE7 32 B2
Providence Pl. DE7 33 C5
Quarry Hill Rd. DE7 33 C8
Queen Elizabeth Way.
  DE7 33 A8
Queen St. DE7 33 C6
Queen Ter. DE7 33 C6
Queens Av. DE7 33 D8
Queens Dri. DE7 33 B6
Raleigh St. DE7 33 C6
Rayneham Rd. DE7 32 A2
Redland Clo. DE7 32 B2
Regent St. DE7 33 C7
Repton Dri. DE7 33 E7
Richmond Av. DE7 33 C6
Rigley Av. DE7 32 C5
Risley Ct. DE7 32 C3
Robbinetts La. NG16 33 F5
Roberts St. DE7 33 D7
Rodney Way. DE7 32 C3
Rope Walk. DE7 33 D5

Rose Av. DE7 32 B4
Rossendale. DE7 32 B2
Rowan Clo. DE7 33 C8
Rupert St. DE7 33 D5
Rutland St. DE7 32 C4
Rutland Ter. DE7 32 C4
St Andrews Dri. DE7 33 B6
St James Av. DE7 33 D7
St Johns Dri. DE7 33 D7
St Mary St. DE7 33 C5
St Norbert Dri. DE7 33 B8
Scarborough Av. DE7 33 B5
Seaford Way. DE7 32 C1
Second Av. DE7 33 C7
Shakespeare Rd. NG16 32 F1
Shaw St. DE7 33 D7
Shepton Clo. DE7 33 A8
Shipley Common La.
  DE7 32 A2
Skeavingtons La. DE7 32 B1
Skipton Clo. DE7 32 A3
Smedley Av. DE7 33 D7
Soloman Rd. DE7 32 E4
South St. DE7 33 C6
Spinney Rd. DE7 33 B7
Spring Garden Ter.
  DE7 32 C4
Springfield Gdn. DE7 32 C4
Stamford St,
  Awsworth. NG16 32 F2
Stamford St,
  Ilkeston. DE7 33 C5
Stanhope St. DE7 33 D8
Stanley Clo. DE7 33 B7
Stanley St. DE7 33 C7
Stanton Rd. DE7 33 C7
Stapleton Rd. DE7 32 B3
Station Clo. DE7 33 C5
Station Rd,
  Awsworth. NG16 32 F1
Station Rd,
  Ilkeston. DE7 33 C5
Station St. DE7 32 D4
Stoney La. DE7 33 E8
Stoppard Clo. DE7 32 A4
Stratford St. DE7 32 C2
Sudbury Av. DE7 33 D6
Summerfields Way.
  DE7 32 A3
Summerfields Way Sth.
  DE7 32 A4
Sycamore Rd. NG16 32 F2
Talbot Pl. DE7 32 C4
Tathams La. DE7 32 C4
Taylor St. DE7 33 C5
Tennyson Sq. NG16 32 F2
Tennyson St. DE7 32 B3
The Copse. DE7 32 A1
The Forge. DE7 33 E8
The Glebe. NG16 32 E2
The Lane. NG16 32 F2
The Triangle. DE7 33 D8
The Vale. DE7 32 B3
Third Av. DE7 33 C7
Thorpe St. DE7 33 D7
Thurman St. DE7 33 D8
Tressall Clo. DE7 33 D6
Trinity Clo. DE7 32 B3
Trinity St. DE7 32 C4
Trowell Av. DE7 33 D8
Truemans Yard. DE7 33 C6
Truman St,
  Cotmanhay. DE7 32 C2
Truman St,
  Ilkeston. DE7 33 D5
Tulip Rd. NG16 32 E2
Turnberry Clo. DE7 32 A4
Union Rd. DE7 33 C7
Valley Rd. DE7 33 B8
Valley Vw. DE7 33 B8
Vernon St. DE7 32 C2
Vicarage Av. DE7 32 B2
Vicarage St. DE7 32 B2
Victoria St. DE7 32 C3
Vincent Av. DE7 33 C6
Vine Farm Clo. DE7 33 A8
Wade Av. DE7 33 D6
Walnut Clo. DE7 33 D7
Wardlow Rd. DE7 32 B3
Weaver Row. DE7 33 C6
Welbeck Av. DE7 33 A8
Wentworth St. DE7 32 D4
Wesley St. DE7 33 C6
West End Cres. DE7 33 A6

West End Dri. DE7 33 A6
West St. DE7 33 C6
West Ter. DE7 33 C6
Westby La. NG16 32 F2
Westfield Dri. DE7 32 A4
Westwick St. DE7 33 B6
White Lion Sq. DE7 33 C6
Whitemead Clo. DE7 32 A4
Whitworth Rd. DE7 33 C7
Willoughby St. DE7 33 D5
Wilmot St. DE7 33 B5
Wilton Pl. DE7 33 C5
Wilton St. DE7 33 C5
Winchester Cres. DE7 33 D6
Windley Dri. DE7 32 A3
Windsor Clo. DE7 33 F8
Wingfield Dri. DE7 33 C5
Wood St. DE7 32 A3
Woodland Clo. DE7 32 A2
Woodside Cres. DE7 32 A1
Wordsworth Rd. NG16 32 F2
Wortley Clo. DE7 33 D6
Wynnard Clo. DE7 32 A3

KILLAMARSH

Acacia Cres. S31 34 B3
Acer Clo. S31 34 B3
Aldred Clo. S31 34 E1
Almond Dri. S31 34 B3
Ash Clo. S31 34 B4
Ashley Clo. S31 34 C3
Ashley La. S31 34 D3
Ashton Clo. S31 34 B3
Aspen Clo. S31 34 B3
Bailey Dri. S31 34 E1
Baker Dri. S31 34 B3
Barbers La. S31 34 D1
Bay Ct. S31 34 D1
Bedgrave Clo. S31 34 E1
Beech Cres. S31 34 C4
Belklane Dri. S31 34 D2
Betony Clo. S31 34 B4
Birch Clo. S31 34 B4
Birchlands Dri. S31 34 D3
Boiley La. S31 34 D4
Briars Clo. S31 34 D4
Bridge St. S31 34 C2
Brindley Ct. S31 34 B3
Bryon Clo. S31 34 B3
Bunkers Hill. S31 34 D3
Butler Way. S31 34 B2
Campion Dri. S31 34 B3
Canal Br. S31 34 C3
Cedar Clo. S31 34 B4
Chandos Cres. S31 34 C3
Cherry Tree Dri. S31 34 C4
Chestnut Av. S31 34 B3
Church La. S31 34 D2
Church Mews. S31 34 D2
Church View. S31 34 D2
Cinder La. S31 34 E2
Cross St. S31 34 E2
Curzon Clo. S31 34 C3
Cutler Clo. S31 34 B2
Cypress Clo. S31 34 C3
Dale Rd. S31 34 D2
Dawber La. S31 34 E2
Delves Rd. S31 34 C3
Dumbleton Rd. S31 34 D4
Elder Ct. S31 34 B3
Ellisons Rd. S31 34 E1
Elm Clo. S31 34 B4
Elm Dri. S31 34 B4
Fanny Av. S31 34 D4
Field La. S31 34 A3
Fir Pl. S31 34 B4
Forge La. S31 34 A2
Foxcroft Chase. S31 34 B3
Foxcroft Dri. S31 34 B3
Foxcroft Gro. S31 34 B3
Gannow Clo. S31 34 E2
Gorse Dri. S31 34 C4
Green La. S31 34 C4
Havercroft Pl. S31 34 B2
Havercroft Ter. S31 34 B2
Hawthorn Clo. S31 34 B4
Hazel Av. S31 34 B4
Heath Av. S31 34 C3
High St. S31 34 C3
Holly Clo. S31 34 B4
Hut La. S31 34 E4

Ivyside Clo. S31 34 D3
Ivyside Gdns. S31 34 D3
Jubilee Cres. S31 34 D2
Juniper Rise. S31 34 B4
Kestrel Clo. S31 34 B2
Killamarsh La. S31 34 F3
Kirkcroft Av. S31 34 D2
Kirkcroft Clo. S31 34 D2
Kirkcroft La. S31 34 C3
Laburnam Gro. S31 34 B4
Larch Av. S31 34 B4
Laurel Dri. S31 34 B4
Lime Tree Av. S31 34 B4
Lipp Av. S31 34 B3
Long La. S31 34 E2
Longacre Way. S20 34 A1
Mallard Dri. S31 34 B3
Mallinder Clo. S31 34 D3
Manor Rd. S31 34 D4
Mansfield Rd. S31 34 B4
Maple Dri. S31 34 B4
Marrison Dri. S31 34 B3
Metcalfe Av. S31 34 B2
Meynell Way. S31 34 B3
Moss Dri. S31 34 C4
Mulberry Way. S31 34 C4
Munro Clo. S31 34 D3
Murray Rd. S31 34 D3
Musard Way. S31 34 D2
Nether Av. S31 34 C3
Nethergreen Av. S31 34 D2
Nethergreen Gdns. S31 34 D2
Nethermoor Av. S31 34 C2
Nethermoor Clo. S31 34 D2
Nethermoor Dri. S31 34 D2
Nethermoor La. S31 34 C2
Netherthorpe Clo. S31 34 B2
Netherthorpe La. S31 34 B2
New St. S20 34 A1
Norburn Dri. S31 34 C3
North Cres. S31 34 D1
North Valley Way. S20 34 A1
Norwood Cres. S31 34 E2
Norwood Pl. S31 34 E2
Oak Clo. S31 34 B4
Orchard Pl. S31 34 C3
Peacock Clo. S31 34 C2
Pear Tree Clo. S31 34 E2
Peatfield Rd. S31 34 E2
Pine Clo. S31 34 B4
Pingle Rd. S31 34 D2
Poplar Clo. S31 34 B4
Powell Dri. S31 34 B3
Primrose Clo. S31 34 D1
Primrose La. S31 34 D1
Quarry Rd. S31 34 A2
Rectory Gdns. S31 34 C3
Rectory Rd. S31 34 C3
Redwood Av. S31 34 B4
Robinson Way. S31 34 B3
Rose Way. S31 34 C3
Rotherham Clo. S31 34 E1
Rotherham Rd. S31 34 E2
Rotherwood Rd. S31 34 D2
Rowan Tree Clo. S31 34 C4
Rowan Tree Rd. S31 34 B3
Sackerville Ter. S31 34 B2
Sheepcote Rd. S31 34 B3
Sheffield Rd,
Holbrook. S20 34 A2
Sheffield Rd,
Killamarsh. S31 34 A2
Sherwood Rd. S31 34 E1
Simcrest Av. S31 34 C4
South Cres. S31 34 E2
Spruce Rise. S31 34 B3
Stanley St. S31 34 C2
Station Rd. S31 34 B2
Sycamore Dri. S31 34 C4
The Bungalows. S31 34 C2
The Green. S31 34 C4
Upperthorpe Rd. S31 34 D4
Upperthorpe Villas.
S31 34 D4
Valley Dri. S31 34 D2
Valley Rd. S31 34 D2
Walford Rd. S31 34 B3
Walkers La. S31 34 C2
Walnut Dri. S31 34 B4
Westfield Rd. S31 34 C4
Westhorpe Rd. S31 34 C4
Willow Rd. S31 34 B4
Woodall Rd. S31 34 F4
Woodside Av. S31 34 E2
Yew Tree Dri. S31 34 B4

KIRK HALLAM

Abbot Rd. DE7 28 B4
Appleby Clo. DE7 28 B4
Ascot Pl. DE7 28 B5
Avondale Rd. DE7 28 B5
Balmoral Rd. DE7 28 C5
Bankfield Dri. DE7 28 A5
Belvoir Clo. DE7 28 C5
Black Hills Dri. DE7 28 D4
Braefield Clo. DE7 28 B5
Buckminster Rd. DE7 28 B6
Bunting Clo. DE7 28 B4
Chatsworth Pl. DE7 28 B5
Cherrytree Clo. DE7 28 C4
Coniston Dri. DE7 28 C5
Crosshill Dri. DE7 28 B5
Dale Vw. DE7 28 D4
Dallimore Rd. DE7 28 C6
Deepdale Av. DE7 28 C5
Derbyshire Dri. DE7 28 B4
Dumbles Clo. DE7 28 C4
Eaton Av. DE7 28 C4
Eliot Dri. DE7 28 C5
Festival Av. DE7 28 B5
Friars Ct. DE7 28 B4
Glendon Rd. DE7 28 B6
Godfrey Dri. DE7 28 B5
Goodwood Cres. DE7 28 C5
Goole Av. DE7 28 C5
Hardwick Pl. DE7 28 B5
Hemlock La. DE7 28 C5
Henshaw Av. DE7 28 C5
Highfield Dri. DE7 28 A5
Hillary Pl. DE7 28 A5
Hobson Dri. DE7 28 D4
INDUSTRIAL ESTATES:
Quarry Hill
Ind Park. DE7 28 D6
Kenilworth Dri. DE7 28 B5
Keswick Clo. DE7 28 C5
Ladywood Rd. DE7 28 A5
Lime Tree Rise. DE7 28 B4
Little Hallam Hill. DE7 28 D5
Lock Clo. DE7 28 B5
Macdonald Sq. DE7 28 B5
Marshall Way. DE7 28 B4
Meerbrook Pl. DE7 28 B5
Nursery Hollow. DE7 28 D4
Nutbrook Cres. DE7 28 C6
Nuthall Circle. DE7 28 B6
Oliver Rd. DE7 28 B5
Poplar Way. DE7 28 C5
Priory Dri. DE7 28 B4
Quarry Hill Rd. DE7 28 D5
Queen Elizabeth Way.
DE7 28 B5
Ribblesdale. DE7 28 B5
Ridgeway Dri. DE7 28 A5
St Norbert Dri. DE7 28 B5
Sandringham Pl. DE7 28 C5
Sharp Clo. DE7 28 B4
Spinney Rd. DE7 28 D4
Sunningdale Dri. DE7 28 A5
Tilton Gro. DE7 28 B6
Trent Rd. DE7 28 C6
Tudor Pl. DE7 28 B5
Valley Rd. DE7 28 D5
Valley Vw. DE7 28 C5
Vine Farm Clo. DE7 28 C5
Welbeck Av. DE7 28 C5
Westfield Clo. DE7 28 B5
Windermere Av. DE7 28 B6
Windsor Cres. DE7 28 C6
Wirksworth Rd. DE7 28 A5
Woolsthorpe Cres. DE7 28 B6
Wyndale Dri. DE7 28 B4

LONG EATON/ BREASTON

Abbott St. NG10 37 F5
Acton Av. NG10 37 H5
Acton Clo. NG10 37 H5
Acton Gro. NG10 37 H5
Acton Rd. NG10 37 H4
Acton St. NG10 37 H5
Adrian Clo. NG9 37 H2
Airedale Clo. NG10 36 D5
Albert Rd. NG10 37 G4
Albion Rd. NG10 37 H3
Aldridge Clo. NG9 37 G1
Alexandra Rd. NG10 37 G3
Ash Gro. DE7 37 E5
Ashview Clo. NG10 36 D3
Austen Av. NG10 37 E6
Avondale Clo. NG10 36 D5
Bakewell Rd. NG10 37 G6
Bank St. NG10 37 G4
Banks Rd. NG9 37 G1
Baslow Clo. NG10 36 C6
Beaconsfield St. NG10 37 G4
Beech Av,
Breaston. DE72 36 C3
Beech Av,
Long Eaton. NG10 37 H3
Belmont Av. DE72 36 B3
Belvoir Clo. NG10 37 G6
Bennett St. NG10 37 E1
Beresford Rd. NG10 36 C6
Berkeley Av. NG10 37 E5
Berwin Clo. NG10 36 D2
Birchwood Av,
Breaston. DE72 36 C4
Birchwood Av,
Long Eaton. NG10 37 E6
Bishopsdale Clo. NG10 36 C5
Bispham Dri. NG9 37 H1
Blake Ct. NG10 36 D6
Blandford Av. NG10 36 D6
Blind La. DE72 36 A3
Bonsall St. NG10 37 H3
Borrowdale Dri. NG10 36 D5
Bostocks La. NG10 36 D1
Bosworth Way. NG10 37 G6
Bothe Clo. NG10 37 E5
Bourne Sq. DE72 36 A4
Bracken Clo. NG10 36 D2
Bracken Rd. NG10 36 D2
Bradshaw St. NG10 37 E6
Bramble Clo. NG10 36 D2
Bransdale Clo. NG10 36 D5
Bredon Clo. NG10 36 D3
Breedon St. NG10 37 E1
Brendon Way. NG10 36 D2
Briar Av. NG10 36 D1
Briar Gate. NG10 36 D1
Bridge St. NG10 37 F3
Brittania Rd. NG10 37 F2
Broad St. NG10 37 G4
Broadstairs Rd. NG9 37 H1
Bronte Clo. NG10 36 D4
Brook Clo. NG10 37 G6
Brookside Clo. NG10 36 D3
Browns Rd. NG10 37 G4
Burlington Clo. DE72 36 A3
Bushy Clo. NG10 37 F5
Buttermere Clo. NG10 36 D1
Cairnsmore Clo. NG10 36 D2
Calderdale Dri. NG10 36 D5
Canal St. NG10 37 F2
Carlin Clo. DE72 36 B3
Carlton Rd. NG10 37 E6
Carrfield Av. NG9 37 H2
Carter Clo. NG10 36 D4
Cavendish Rd. NG10 37 E1
Cedar Av. NG10 37 F6
Chapel St. NG10 37 G4
Charles St. NG10 37 F5
Cheapside Clo. NG10 36 D3
Cheltenham Clo. NG9 37 H2
Cherry Clo. DE72 36 B3
Chesterfield Av. NG10 37 H4
Cheviot Rd. NG10 36 D2
Chiltern Gdns. NG10 36 D2
Church Vw. NG10 36 A3
Churchill Clo. DE72 36 A3
Clay St. NG10 37 G4
Cleveland Av. NG9 37 H3
Clifford St. NG10 37 G4
Clumber St. NG10 37 F4
Cobden St. NG10 37 F5
Cockleys. NG10 37 F5
College St. NG10 37 E1
Collingwood Rd. NG10 37 G5
Coniston Clo. NG10 36 D1
Conway St. NG10 37 H3
Co-operative St. NG10 37 G5
Cooke Clo. NG10 36 D4
Copeside Clo. NG10 36 D3
Cornwallis Clo. NG10 37 G5
Cotswold Clo. NG10 36 D3
Craig St. NG10 37 G4
Cranfleet Way. NG10 36 D4
Cranmer St. NG10 37 G3

Cromford Clo. NG10 36 C6
Crowcroft Way. NG10 37 E1
Cross St. NG10 37 G3
Crown Clo. NG10 36 D4
Crowcroft Way. NG10 37 E1
Cuillin Clo. NG10 36 D2
Curzon St. NG10 37 E1
Dale Av. NG10 37 G2
Darley Dri. NG10 36 D6
Darwin Rd. NG10 37 E6
Denacre Av. NG9 37 H2
Deepdale Rd. NG10 36 D6
Delamere Clo. DE72 36 A3
Derby Rd. NG10 36 D3
Derwent St. NG10 37 E5
Dockholm Rd. NG10 37 E1
Doncaster Gro. NG9 37 H2
Douglas Rd. NG10 37 E2
Dove La. NG10 37 F3
Dovedale Av. NG10 36 D5
Dovedale Ct. NG10 37 E5
Draycott Rd. NG10 36 C6
Duffield Clo. NG10 36 C6
Earlswood Clo. DE72 36 A3
East St. NG10 37 H3
Eaton Grange Dri.
NG10 36 D3
Edale Clo. NG10 37 E5
Edge Hill Clo. NG10 37 G4
Edward Rd. NG10 37 G4
Elgar Dri. NG10 36 D6
Eliot Clo. NG10 37 E6
Ellis Clo. NG10 37 E5
Elm Av. NG10 37 F3
Ennerdale Rd. NG10 37 E1
Erdington Way. NG9 37 G1
Erewash Gro. NG9 37 H2
Eskdale Clo. NG10 36 D6
Fair Lea Clo. NG10 37 F5
Far Croft. DE72 36 A3
Farm Clo. NG10 37 G6
Farndale Clo. NG10 36 D6
Farthing Ct. NG10 36 D4
Fearn Clo. DE72 36 C4
Ferndene Dri. NG10 36 D5
Field Clo. DE72 36 C4
Fields Farm Rd. NG10 37 G5
Firfield Av. DE72 36 B3
Fletcher St. NG10 37 G4
Florence Av. NG9 37 H2
Florin Gdns. NG10 36 D4
Forbes Clo. NG10 37 G6
Fosbrooke Dri. NG10 37 G6
Fox Clo. NG10 37 F6
Frederick St. NG10 37 H4
Freeland Clo. NG9 37 H1
Friar St. NG10 37 F4
Frisby Av. NG10 37 G5
Fulwood Dri. NG10 36 D4
Fylde Clo. NG10 37 H1
Gainsboro Clo. NG10 37 G6
George Av. NG9 37 H3
Gibb St. NG10 37 G4
Gladstone St. NG10 37 F5
Glenfield Rd. NG10 37 F6
Goodwood Dri. NG9 37 H1
Gorse Clo. NG10 37 E1
Grampian Way. NG10 36 D3
Grange Av. DE72 36 A3
Grange Dri. NG10 37 H3
Granville Av. NG10 37 G5
Grasmere Rd. NG10 36 D1
Greenside Clo. NG10 37 H4
Grosvenor Av. DE72 36 B3
Grosvenor Rd. NG10 36 D6
Guinea Clo. NG10 36 D4
Hadleigh Clo. NG9 37 G1
Hambleton Clo. NG10 36 D2
Hamilton Clo. NG9 37 H1
Hamilton Rd. NG10 37 F5
Hardy Clo. NG10 37 G5
Harrimans Dri. DE72 36 C3
Hartside Gdns. NG10 36 D2
Haslemere Rd. NG10 37 E3
Hathern Clo. NG10 37 E1
Hathersage Av. NG10 36 C6
Hatton Cres. NG10 37 G5
Hawthorne Av. DE72 36 C3
Hawthorne Rd. NG10 37 G5
Heath Gdns. DE72 36 C3
Heather Cres. DE72 36 C4
Helvellyn Way. NG10 37 E1
Hemlock Av. NG10 37 G2
High Croft. DE72 36 C3
High St. NG10 37 G6

Highfield St. NG10 37 F2
Hillside Dri. NG10 36 D3
Holland Mdw. NG10 37 F6
Holly Av. DE72 36 C2
Holmes Rd. DE72 36 A3
Holyoake Dri. NG10 37 H4
Hooley Clo. NG10 37 E5
Hoselett Field Rd. NG10 37 G6
Howard Clo. NG10 37 G2
Howarth Clo. NG10 36 C4
Howitt St. NG10 37 E2
Humber Rd. NG10 37 E2
Huntingdon Way. NG9 37 H1
Huss's La. NG10 37 H4
Ingham Rd. NG10 37 E1
Ingleborough Gdns. NG10 36 D3
Keats Clo. NG10 37 E5
Kedleston Clo. NG10 36 C6
Kendal Rd. NG10 37 E1
Kennedy Av. NG10 37 E6
Keswick Clo. NG10 36 D1
King St. NG10 37 F3
Kingsdale Clo. NG10 36 C6
Kirkdale Gdns. NG10 36 D6
Kirkdale Rd. NG10 36 D6
Kirkfield Dri. DE72 36 A3
Kirkham Dri. NG9 37 H1
Kirkstone Ct. NG10 37 E1
Kirkwhite Av. NG10 37 G4
Kirton Av. NG10 37 G4
Lakeside Cres. NG10 37 F6
Laneside Av. NG9 37 G1
Langdale Dri. NG10 36 C5
Langdon Clo. NG10 36 D2
Lansdown Gro. NG9 37 H2
Lathkilldale Cres. NG10 36 D6
Laurel Cres. NG10 37 E5
Lawrence Av. DE72 36 A3
Lawrence St. NG10 37 G3
Lawson Av. NG10 37 G4
Leicester St. NG10 37 G5
Leigh Rd. NG9 37 H1
Leopold St. NG10 37 F3
Leyland Clo. NG9 37 H1
Lime Gro. NG10 37 F3
Lime Ter. NG10 37 F3
Lodge Rd. NG10 37 F6
Longmoor Gdns. NG10 36 D1
Longmoor La. DE72 36 A3
Longmoor Rd. NG10 36 D1
Lonsdale Dri. NG9 37 G1
Lower Brook St. NG10 37 G4
Lynden Av. NG10 37 F5
Lyndhurst Gro. NG10 37 F2
Main St, Breaston. DE72 36 A4
Main St, Long Eaton. NG10 37 H4
Malvern Gdns. NG10 36 D3
Manchester St. NG10 37 F5
Mannion Cres. NG10 36 D6
Manor Ct. DE72 36 A3
Manor House Rd. NG10 37 H5
Manorleigh. DE72 36 A3
Maple Gro. DE72 36 C4
Margaret Av. NG9 37 H2
Market Pl. NG10 37 G3
Marlborough Rd, Breaston. DE72 36 A4
Marlborough Rd, Long Eaton. NG9 37 H3
Matlock Ct. NG10 36 C6
Maxwell St, Breaston. DE72 36 B4
Maxwell St, Long Eaton. NG10 37 G4
Mayfield Gro. NG9 37 H2
Maylands Av. DE72 36 B3
Meadow Clo. DE72 36 B4
Meadow La. NG10 37 H4
Mendip Clo. NG10 36 D2
Meynell Rd. NG10 37 G6
Mickledon Clo. NG10 36 D1
Midland St. NG10 37 G3
Mikado Rd. NG10 37 E6
Mill Hill La. DE72 36 A2
Milldale Rd. NG10 36 D5
Milner Rd. NG10 37 F2
Milton St. NG10 37 G4

Mint Clo. NG10 36 D4
Mitchell St. NG10 37 G4
Monsaldale Clo. NG10 36 D5
Moorlands Clo. NG10 36 D1
Mount St. DE72 36 B4
Myrtle Av. NG10 37 E5
Naseby Dri. NG10 37 G6
Nathaniel Rd. NG10 37 G4
Neale St. NG10 37 G4
Near Meadow. NG10 37 G6
Neighwood Clo. NG9 37 G1
Nelson St. NG10 37 F5
New St. NG10 37 G3
New Tythe St. NG10 37 H4
Newmarket Way. NG9 37 H2
Norfolk Rd. NG9 37 H3
North Rd. NG10 37 F5
Northcote St. NG10 37 G4
Nottingham Rd. NG10 37 G3
Oakland Av. NG10 37 F6
Oakland Ter. NG10 37 F6
Oakleys Rd. NG10 37 G4
Oakleys Rd West. NG10 37 G5
Olive Av. NG10 37 G2
Orchard Clo. DE72 36 B3
Orchard St. NG10 37 G4
Orchard Way. NG10 36 D1
Orpean Way. NG9 37 H1
Osmaston Clo. NG10 36 C6
Overdale Clo. NG10 36 C5
Oxford St. NG10 37 G3
Ozier Holt. NG10 37 F5
Paddocks Vw. NG10 36 D3
Park Dri. NG10 36 D1
Park St, Breaston. DE72 36 B3
Park St, Long Eaton. NG10 37 F2
Parkside Av. NG10 36 D3
Peakdale Clo. NG10 36 D5
Peel St. NG10 37 G3
Penine Clo. NG10 36 D2
Penmoor Clo. NG10 36 D5
Pennie Clo. NG10 37 G6
Pennyfields Blvd. NG10 36 D4
Pentland Gdns. NG10 36 D2
Petersgate. NG10 36 D2
Petersgate Clo. NG10 36 D2
Petersham Rd. NG10 36 D2
Peveril Cres. NG10 36 C6
Phyllis Gro. NG10 37 H4
Plackett Clo. DE72 36 A3
Poplar Rd. DE72 36 B2
Porlock Clo. NG10 36 D2
Portland Rd. NG9 37 F3
Prince St. NG10 37 F3
Princess St. NG10 37 F3
Purbeck Clo. NG10 36 D3
Purdy Meadow. NG10 36 C6
Pym Leys. NG10 36 C6
Quantock Rd. NG10 36 D2
Queen St. NG10 37 G4
Quorndon Cres. NG10 37 F6
Rad Mdws. NG10 37 F6
Raeburn Dri. NG9 37 G1
Ravensdale Av. NG10 36 E1
Recreation St. NG10 37 H3
Regent St. NG10 37 G4
Ribblesdale Rd. NG10 36 C6
Riber Clo. NG10 37 F6
Richmond Av. DE72 36 C3
Risley La. DE72 36 A1
Rivington Rd. NG10 37 H1
Rochester Clo. NG10 36 D4
Roosevelt Av. NG10 37 E6
Rose Ct. NG10 37 E3
Rosedale Clo. NG10 36 D5
Rowsley Av. NG10 36 C6
Royal Av. NG10 37 F2
Rufford Rd. NG10 37 D6
Rush Leys. NG10 37 G6
Ruskin Av. NG10 36 D6
Russell St. NG10 37 F2
Rydal Av. NG10 36 D1
St Johns St. NG10 37 G4
St Laurence Ct. NG10 37 G5
St Vincents Clo. NG10 37 G5
Salisbury St. NG10 37 G4
Sandfield Rd. NG9 37 G1
Sandford Av. NG10 37 H3
Sandown Rd. NG10 37 H1
Sandwell Clo. NG10 36 D5

Sawley Rd. DE72 36 B4
Sawmand Clo. NG10 37 F5
Seaburn Rd. NG9 37 G1
Shakespeare St. NG10 37 F2
Sharpe Clo. NG10 37 E5
Sheriffs Lea. NG9 37 G1
Shilling Way. NG10 36 D4
Sidney St. NG10 37 F5
South St. NG10 37 G4
Southfields. NG10 37 G4
Sovereign Gro. NG10 36 D4
Spinney Cres. NG9 37 H1
Spinney Dri. NG10 37 E1
Spinney Rd. NG10 37 E1
*Spridgeon Clo, Moorlands Clo. NG10 36 D1
Springfield Av. NG10 37 H3
Stafford St. NG10 37 H3
Stamford Clo. NG10 35 G6
Stanhope St. NG10 37 F3
Stanley St. NG10 37 F3
Stapleford La. NG9 37 H1
Station Rd. NG10 37 H3
Station St. NG10 37 H4
Sterndale Rd. NG10 36 D5
Stevens La. DE72 36 A3
Stone Mdws. NG10 37 G6
Stourdale Clo. NG10 36 C5
Stridingedge Clo. NG10 37 E1
Sycamore Rd. NG10 37 E6
Tamworth Rd. NG10 37 E6
Teesdale Rd. NG10 36 D6
Tenter Clo. NG10 37 F6
Tewkesbury Rd. NG10 37 G6
The Chestnuts. NG10 36 D3
The Grove. DE72 36 B3
The Pingle. NG10 37 F3
The Plantations. NG10 36 D3
The Spring. NG10 37 F6
The Watermeadows. NG10 36 D3
Thirlmere Clo. NG10 36 D1
Thirlmere Rd. NG10 36 D1
Thoresby Rd. NG10 37 E5
Thorneywood Rd. NG10 37 H3
Thorntree Clo. DE72 36 B3
Thorpe Leys. NG10 37 G6
Trafalgar Rd. NG10 37 G5
Trafalgar Sq. NG10 37 H4
*Trafalgar Ter, Trafalgar Sq. NG10 37 H4
Trent La. NG10 37 H6
Trent St. NG10 37 G3
Trowell Gro. NG10 37 E2
Tudor Clo. NG10 37 G2
Tynedale Clo. NG10 36 C5
Union St. NG10 37 G3
Upper Wellington St. NG10 37 F2
Vanguard Rd. NG10 37 G6
Victoria St. NG10 36 D6
Victory Clo. NG10 37 G1
Vyse Dri. NG10 37 E5
Walton St. NG10 37 G3
Wards La. DE72 36 A3
Waverley Av. NG10 37 E1
Wellington St. NG10 37 E1
Wensleydale Rd. NG10 36 D5
West Gate. NG10 37 F2
Westdale Clo. NG10 36 D6
Westhorpe Dri. NG10 37 E3
Wharfedale Rd. NG10 36 C5
Whitburn Rd. NG9 37 G1
Whiting Av. NG9 37 H1
William St. NG10 37 E1
Willoughby Av. NG10 37 E1
Willoughby Clo. DE72 36 B3
Willow Av. NG10 37 G2
Wilmot St. NG10 36 C6
Wilsthorpe Rd. DE72 36 B3
*Windermere Gdns, Windermere Rd. NG10 36 D1
Windermere Rd. NG10 36 D1
Winster Way. NG10 36 C6
Wittering Clo. NG10 37 G6
Woodland Av. DE72 36 C3
Woodside Cres. NG10 37 E3
Worral Av. NG10 37 G2
Wyvern Av. NG10 37 F5
York Rd. NG10 37 F2

MATLOCK

Acorn Ridge. DE4 38 C2
Alders La. DE4 39 H6
Alfreton Rd. DE4 39 E5
All Saints Rd. DE4 38 C3
Allen Hill. DE4 38 C3
Alton Rise. DE4 38 A2
Amberdene. DE4 39 E3
Amecroft La. DE4 38 B1
Ashley Clo. DE4 39 H5
Asker La. DE4 39 E3
Bakewell Rd. DE4 38 A1
Bank Rd Gdns. DE4 38 D3
Bank Rd. DE4 38 D4
Bent La. DE4 38 D2
Bentley Clo. DE4 39 E2
Bidston Clo. DE4 38 D2
Blackrocks Av. DE4 38 A2
Boam La. DE4 38 B1
Brook Lea. DE4 38 D5
Brookfield Way. DE4 39 G5
Bull La. DE4 39 F3
Burnett La. DE4 38 B1
Butts Dri. DE4 39 E5
Carr La. DE4 39 H6
Carson Croft. DE4 38 D4
Causeway La. DE4 38 D4
Cavendish Rd. DE4 38 D2
Chatsworth Rd. DE4 38 A2
Chesterfield Rd. DE4 39 E4
Church St, Matlock. DE4 38 D5
Church St, Tansley Knoll. DE4 39 H4
Cleve Av. DE4 38 B2
Cobden Rd. DE4 38 D3
Collingwood Cres. DE4 38 B3
Crook Stile. DE4 38 C2
Crown Sq. DE4 38 C4
Cunnery La. DE4 39 H6
Dale Rd. DE4 38 C4
Dale Rd South. DE4 38 A1
Dales Field. DE4 38 B3
Darley House Est. DE4 38 A3
Days Mill Clo. DE4 38 B3
Deep Carr La. DE4 39 E5
Dene Fields Ct. DE4 38 D4
Devonshire Rd. DE4 38 B2
Dimple Cres. DE4 38 C3
Dimple Rd. DE4 38 C3
Drabbles Rd. DE4 38 C3
Edge Rd. DE4 38 C3
Edgefold Rd. DE4 38 D4
Elm Av. DE4 38 B2
Fairholmes. DE4 39 E4
Far Cross. DE4 38 D2
Far Green. DE4 38 C3
Farley Hill. DE4 38 B1
Farm La. DE4 39 E3
Firs Par. DE4 38 C3
Foxholes La. DE4 39 G2
George Rd. DE4 38 C3
Goldhill. DE4 39 H5
Green Clo. DE4 38 C3
Green La. DE4 39 H4
Gritstone Rd. DE4 39 E2
Grove La. DE4 38 A1
Hackney Rd. DE4 38 B1
Hawleys Clo. DE4 39 F3
Hazel Gro. DE4 39 E4
Heathfield Av. DE4 38 D2
Henry Av. DE4 38 D3
High Ridge. DE4 38 D2
Highfield Dri. DE4 39 E3
Hill Tops Vw. DE4 39 E4
Holly La. DE4 39 H5
Holmesfield Clo. DE4 39 H4
Holt Dri. DE4 38 B3
Holt La. DE4 38 C4
Hopewell Rd. DE4 38 D3
Hurds Hollow. DE4 38 B2
Hurker Rise. DE4 39 E4
Hurst Rise. DE4 39 E4
Imperial Rd. DE4 38 C3
INDUSTRIAL ESTATES:
Brookfield Park Ind Est. DE4 39 G5
Jackson Rd. DE4 38 C3
Jackson Tor Rd. DE4 38 C3
John St. DE4 38 C3

Knowlstone Pl. DE4 38 D5
Lily Bank Clo. DE4 38 D4
Lime Grove Av. DE4 38 D4
Lime Grove Walk. DE4 38 D4
Lime Tree Rd. DE4 38 D5
Linden Gro. DE4 39 E4
Lonsdale Gro. DE4 38 A2
Lumsdale. DE4 39 F2
Lumsdale Cres. DE4 39 E4
Lumsdale Rd. DE4 39 F3
Lumshill Rise. DE4 39 E3
Lynholmes Rise. DE4 39 E4
Lynholmes Rd. DE4 39 E4
Malpas Rd. DE4 38 C3
Malvern Gdns. DE4 38 D3
Maple View. DE4 38 D6
Matlock Green. DE4 38 D5
Megdale. DE4 38 B3
Mettesford. DE4 39 E4
Mews Ct. DE4 39 H4
Mias Clo. DE4 39 H4
Mooredge Dri. DE4 39 F3
Moorfield. DE4 38 D2
Mornington Rise. DE4 39 E5
New St. DE4 38 D4
Oak Rd. DE4 39 H5
Oak Tree Gdns. DE4 39 H5
Oaksedge La. DE4 39 H3
Old Coach Rd. DE4 39 G5
Old Hackney La. DE4 38 A1
Old Lime Ct. DE4 39 E4
Olde Englishe Rd. DE4 38 D5
Orchard La. DE4 38 A1
Overdale. DE4 39 F4
Paxton Clo. DE4 38 B3
Pic Tor La. DE4 38 D5
Pinewood Rd. DE4 38 D2
Pope Carr Rd. DE4 38 D4
Prospect Dri. DE4 38 C3
Pump Clo. DE4 38 D6
Quarry Bank. DE4 38 C2
Quarry La. DE4 39 F2
Riber Clo. DE4 39 H4
Riber Rd. DE4 39 F6
Riber View. DE4 39 H4
Rockside Vw. DE4 38 D2
Rutland Av. DE4 38 D3
Rutland St. DE4 38 C4
St Giles Walk. DE4 38 D5
St Johns Rd. DE4 38 C6
St Joseph St. DE4 38 D4
Salters La. DE4 38 A5
Sandy La. DE4 39 E2
School Rd. DE4 39 E4
Sheriff Dri. DE4 38 C3
Sheriff La. DE4 38 B3
Sherwood Rd. DE4 39 E5
Smedley St. DE4 38 C3
Smedley St East. DE4 38 D3
Smedley St West. DE4 38 C2
Smith Rd. DE4 38 D3
Smuse La. DE4 39 F5
Snitterton Rd. DE4 38 A4
South View. DE4 39 H5
Springfield Rise. DE4 39 E3
Stanton Moor Vw. DE4 38 A2
Starkholmes Rd. DE4 38 D4
Steep Turnpike. DE4 38 D4
Stoney Way. DE4 38 D5
Sycamore Rd. DE4 38 C3
Tawney Clo. DE4 39 H5
Thatchers La. DE4 39 H6
The Close. DE4 39 H4
The Croft. DE4 39 H4
The Knoll. DE4 39 H4
The Limes Clo. DE4 39 E4
The Rocks. DE4 39 H4
The Shortlands. DE4 38 D5
Tor Rise. DE4 38 D6
Turnpike Clo. DE4 39 E4
Victoria Hall Gdns. DE4 38 D3
Wellfield Ct. DE4 39 E3
Wellington Clo. DE4 39 E2
Wellington St. DE4 38 D3
West Cres. DE4 38 B2
Whitelea La. DE4 39 H4
Whitewood Way. DE4 38 C3
Wilmot St. DE4 38 C3
Wishing Stone Way. DE4 39 F3
Wolds Rise. DE4 38 D2
Woolley Rd. DE4 38 C3
Wyvern Clo. DE4 38 C3

Copse Wood. DE55 45 A3
Corn Clo. DE55 45 C2
Corn Dri. DE55 45 C2
Cornfield Av. DE55 45 A4
Coronation Dri. DE55 45 B3
Croft Clo. NG16 45 C4
Dahlia Clo. DE55 45 B1
Dalewood Clo. DE55 45 A4
Downing St. DE55 45 B1
Duke St. DE55 45 B2
Eastfield Dri. DE55 45 B2
Elm Clo. NG16 45 D5
Elmhurst Av. DE55 45 A3
Elmhurst Clo. DE55 45 A3
Erica Dri. DE55 45 B1
Field La. DE55 45 A1
Field View. DE55 45 A1
Fordbridge La. DE55 45 A1
George St. NG16 45 C4
Gladstone St. DE55 45 B2
Glebe Clo. DE55 45 B3
Gordon Cres. DE55 45 B4
Gray Fallow. DE55 45 C4
Greenacres Dri. DE55 45 B1
Hamlet La. DE55 45 A2
Hammer Leys. DE55 45 C4
Hardie Av. DE55 45 A2
Hastlewell Flat. DE55 45 C4
Hawthorne Rd. NG16 45 D5
Hawthornes Av. DE55 45 A3
Hayes. NG16 45 C4
Hazel Gro. DE55 45 C3
Heather Clo. DE55 45 B4
High St. DE55 45 A2
High View Rd. DE55 45 C1
Highfield Dri. DE55 45 B2
Hilcote St. DE55 45 A1
Hill Fields. DE55 45 A4
Hillcrest Av. DE55 45 A4
Hilltop Rd. NG16 45 C4
Hollyhouse Dri. DE55 45 B1
Kennack Clo. DE55 45 D2
King St,
  Pinxton. NG16 45 D4
King St, South
  Normanton. DE55 45 A3
Kirkstead Clo. NG16 45 D5
Kirkstead Rd. NG16 45 D5
Kynance Clo. DE55 45 D2
Laburnum Clo. DE55 45 B1
Lambcroft Rd. NG16 45 D4
Lansbury Dri. DE55 45 A2
Larchdale Clo. DE55 45 B4
Larkspur Clo. DE55 45 A4
Laurel Gro. DE55 45 A3
Lea Bank. DE55 45 B4
Lea Vale. DE55 45 B4
Leamington Dri. DE55 45 B3
Lees La. DE55 45 A2
Lilac Ct. DE55 45 A3
Lilac Clo. DE55 45 A3
Lime Clo. NG16 45 D5
Lime Gro. DE55 45 B3
Little Breck. DE55 45 B4
Long Sleets. DE55 45 C4
Main St. DE55 45 B1
Mansfield Rd. DE55 45 B4
Maple Dri. DE55 45 B4
Market Av. DE55 45 A2
Market Pl. DE55 45 A2
Market St. DE55 45 A3
Matt Orchard. DE55 45 C4
Meadow Ct. DE55 45 A3
Meadow Bank. DE55 45 A1
Meadow La. DE55 45 A1
Mill Holme. DE55 45 C4
Mill La. NG16 45 D6
Monsal Dri. DE55 45 A3
Mount Cres. DE55 45 A4
New St. DE55 45 A1
Newlyn Dri. DE55 45 C2
Normanton Brook Rd.
  DE55 45 D1
North Clo. DE55 45 A2
North St. DE55 45 A2
Nursery Gdns. DE55 45 C3
Oak Clo. NG16 45 D5
Oakdale Rd. DE55 45 B4
Old Storth La. DE55 45 C3
Paddocks Clo. DE55 45 D3
Paddocks Clo. DE55 45 D3
Park Clo. NG16 45 D6
Park La. NG16 45 D5
Peach Av. DE55 45 B1

Peel St. DE55 45 B2
Pendine Clo. DE55 45 D2
Pennine Dri. DE55 45 A3
Penryn Clo. DE55 45 D2
Pinxton La. DE55 45 C3
Platt St. NG16 45 D5
Pool Clo. NG16 45 D5
Poplar Rd. DE55 45 B1
Princess Av. DE55 45 B2
Prospect Av. DE55 45 A3
Queen St,
  Pinxton. NG16 45 D5
Queen St, South
  Normanton. DE55 45 A3
Red La. DE55 45 A4
Redgate St. NG16 45 D5
Sacheverall Av. NG16 45 D4
St Helens Av. NG16 45 D4
St Michaels Dri. DE55 45 B1
School La. DE55 45 C3
*Silken Holme, The
  Pemberton. DE55 45 B4
Slade Clo. DE55 45 B4
Sleights La. NG16 45 D6
Slough Rd. DE55 45 B1
South St. DE55 45 B2
Southfields Av. NG16 45 D4
Southfields Dri. DE55 45 C3
Sporton Clo. DE55 45 B1
Sporton La. DE55 45 B1
Stormont Clo. DE55 45 B4
Storth La. DE55 45 B3
Storthfield Way. DE55 45 B3
Suff La. NG16 45 C4
Sycamore Clo. NG16 45 D5
Talbot St. NG16 45 D6
The Brockwell. DE55 45 B4
The Brunnen. DE55 45 B4
The Chine. DE55 45 B4
The Common. DE55 45 A3
The Croft. DE55 45 B1
The Duesbury. DE55 45 B1
The Grange. DE55 45 B4
The Hamlet. DE55 45 B2
The Oaklands. DE55 45 B4
The Pemberton. DE55 45 B4
The Sycamores. DE55 45 B3
Town St. NG16 45 D4
Turnley Rd. DE55 45 D2
Union St. DE55 45 A3
Victoria Rd. NG16 45 D4
Victoria St. DE55 45 B1
Water La. DE55 45 B2
West End. DE55 45 C4
West St. DE55 45 A3
Westland Dri. NG16 45 C4
Wharf Rd. DE55 45 D6
Widmerpool St. NG16 45 C6
Willow Clo. DE55 45 B3
York Ter. NG16 45 D6

SPONDON/ OCKBROOK/ BORROWASH

Acorn Way. DE21 46 A3
Albemarle Rd. DE21 46 A1
Albert Cres. DE21 46 A3
Albert Rd. DE21 46 A3
Anglers La. DE21 46 C5
Anne Potter Clo. DE72 47 G2
*Appian Clo,
  Roman Way. DE72 47 F6
Apple Tree Clo. DE72 47 G6
Argyll Clo. DE21 46 D3
Arnhem Ter. DE21 46 C4
Arundel Dri. DE21 46 D3
Ashbrook Av. DE72 47 F5
Ashmeadow. DE72 47 F6
Aspen Dri. DE21 46 A3
Asterdale Vw. DE21 46 D2
Atchison Gdns. DE21 46 A1
Avondale Rd. DE21 46 C2
Ayre Clo. DE21 46 C3
Badger Clo. DE21 46 D1
Bains Dri. DE72 47 G6
Bakehouse La. DE72 47 F3
Ballards Way. DE72 47 G6
Balmoral Rd. DE72 47 F5
Bamburgh Clo. DE21 46 C3
Bankfield Dri. DE21 46 D3

Bare La. DE72 47 F3
Barrons Way. DE72 47 F6
Barton Clo. DE72 47 F6
Beaumaris Ct. DE21 46 D2
Beech Av. DE72 47 F4
Beech Clo. DE21 46 C3
Beeches Av. DE21 46 B3
Belmont Dri. DE72 47 F5
Beresford Dri. DE21 46 D4
Borrow Fields. DE72 47 F6
Borrowash
  By-Pass. DE21 46 B5
Borrowash Rd. DE21 46 D4
Borrowfield Rd. DE21 46 C4
Boston Clo. DE21 46 B2
Brackley Dri. DE21 46 D3
Bradbury. DE72 47 G6
Brecon Clo. DE21 46 C2
Briar Clo,
  Borrowash. DE72 47 F5
Briar Clo,
  Cherrytree Hill. DE21 46 A3
Bridgeport Rd. DE21 46 A2
Brockley. DE21 46 C2
Brook Rd. DE72 47 F6
Brunswood Clo. DE21 46 C2
Burnside Dri. DE21 46 D3
Burrowfield Mews.
  DE21 46 D5
Caernarvon Clo. DE21 46 D2
Cambridge St. DE21 46 C4
Carson Rd. DE21 46 A1
Cavan Clo. DE21 46 A3
Cedar Dri. DE21 46 A3
Celanese Rd. DE21 46 B4
Central Av. DE72 47 F6
Chaffinch Clo. DE21 46 D1
Challis Av. DE21 46 A1
Chapel La. DE21 46 C2
Chapel Row. DE72 47 F5
Chapel Side. DE21 46 C2
Chapel St. DE21 46 C2
Charles Av. DE21 46 C2
Charleston Rd. DE21 46 A2
Charnwood Av. DE72 47 G5
Cherry Tree Mews.
  DE21 46 A3
Chesapeake Rd. DE21 46 A2
Chester Ct. DE21 46 D2
Chesterton Rd. DE21 46 A2
Chestnut Gro. DE72 47 F4
Chevin Av. DE72 47 F5
Cheyenne Gdns. DE21 46 A2
Church Hill. DE21 46 C3
Church Hill Ter. DE21 46 C3
Church Mews. DE21 46 C3
Church St,
  Ockbrook. DE72 47 G3
Church St,
  Spondon. DE21 46 C3
Cleveland Av. DE21 46 A3
Clover Clo. DE21 46 D3
Cock Way. DE21 46 D4
Cole La. DE72 47 G4
Coleraine Clo. DE21 46 A3
Collier La. DE72 47 F4
Collumbell Av. DE72 47 G2
Coniston Av. DE21 46 C2
Conway Av. DE72 47 G5
Coopers Clo. DE72 47 F6
Cordville Clo. DE21 46 A3
Coxon St. DE21 46 C2
Craddock Av. DE21 46 C4
Croft Clo,
  Ockbrook. DE72 47 F3
Croft Clo,
  Spondon. DE21 46 D2
Cumberland Cres.
  DE72 47 E5
Cypress Walk. DE21 46 A3
Dale Rd. DE21 46 D2
Dayton Clo. DE21 46 A2
Deans Dri. DE72 47 F5
Deepdale Av. DE72 47 G5
Deepdale Rd. DE21 46 D4
Deer Park Vw. DE21 46 D1
Deincourt Clo. DE21 46 D2
Denison Gdns. DE21 46 A2
Derby Rd,
  Borrowash. DE72 47 E5
Derby Rd,
  Cherrytree Hill. DE21 46 A3
Derby Rd,
  Shackcross. DE72 47 G6

Derwent Av. DE72 47 G4
Derwent Rise. DE21 46 D3
Derwent Rd. DE21 46 B4
Devas Gdns. DE21 46 B2
Devonshire Av. DE72 47 G5
Dolphin Clo. DE21 47 E1
Dovecot Dri. DE21 47 E5
Dovedale Rd. DE21 46 D4
Draycott Rd. DE72 47 G6
Dreyfus Clo. DE21 46 D2
Drury Av. DE21 46 C4
Eardley Clo. DE21 46 A3
Edal Dri. DE21 46 D4
Eden Rd. DE21 46 A3
Edmund Rd. DE21 46 D4
Elizabeth Clo. DE21 46 A3
Ellendale Rd. DE21 46 A1
Elm Gro. DE21 46 A3
Elm St. DE72 47 F5
Ennis Clo. DE21 46 A4
Enoch Stone Dri. DE21 46 A3
Evanston Gdns. DE21 46 A2
Faires Clo. DE72 47 G6
Fairfield Av. DE72 47 F4
Fallow Rd. DE21 46 D1
Far La. DE72 47 G2
Farningham Clo. DE21 46 D2
Fellside. DE21 46 D2
Field Clo. DE72 47 F4
Flood St. DE72 47 G3
Fosse Clo. DE72 47 F6
Fowler Av. DE21 46 B3
Frazer Clo. DE21 46 D2
Galway Av. DE21 46 A4
Gascoigne Dri. DE21 46 B3
Gerard Clo. DE21 46 D2
Gilbert Clo. DE21 46 C3
Gladstone Rd. DE21 46 C3
Glendale Dri. DE21 46 D2
Goldcrest Dri. DE21 46 D1
*Goldstone Ct,
  Gravel La. DE21 46 D3
Gordon Rd. DE72 47 F6
Grant Av. DE21 46 A2
Grasmere Av. DE21 46 C2
Gravel La. DE21 46 D3
Green Bank. DE21 46 C4
Green La. DE72 47 G2
Greenfinch Clo. DE21 46 D2
Greenway Clo. DE72 47 F4
Gypsy La. DE72 47 H6
Haddon Dri. DE21 46 D4
Hall Dyke. DE21 46 C3
Hamilton Rd. DE21 46 D2
Hampton Clo. DE21 46 A1
Hargrave Av. DE72 47 G2
Harrington Av. DE72 47 G5
Hawthorne Av. DE72 47 F5
Hazel Dri. DE21 47 E2
Hermitage Av. DE72 47 F4
Heronswood Dri. DE21 46 C2
Hill View Gro. DE21 46 A2
Hillcroft Dri. DE72 47 F3
Hillside Cres. DE21 46 A3
Hillside Rd. DE21 46 D3
Holme La. DE21 46 B5
Holyrood Clo. DE72 47 F2
Home Farm Clo. DE72 47 F2
Houston Clo. DE21 46 A2
Huntley Av. DE21 46 D1
Ingle Clo. DE21 46 C3
Jasmine Clo. DE21 46 A3
John Fitzgerald
  Kennedy Gdns. DE21 46 A1
Kildare Rd. DE21 46 A3
Kimberley Rd. DE72 47 F5
Kirk Leys Av Nth. DE21 46 C2
Kirk Leys Av Sth. DE21 46 C4
Kirkdale Clo. DE21 46 D4
Ladybower Rd. DE21 46 C4
Lancaster Walk. DE21 47 E2
Langley Rd. DE21 46 C4
Lansing Gdns. DE21 46 A2
Lawnside. DE21 46 D2
Lawrence Av. DE21 46 A3
Leeway. DE21 46 B4
Lewiston Rd. DE21 46 A3
Lexington Rd. DE21 46 A3
Limerick Rd. DE21 46 A3
Linnet Clo. DE21 46 D1
Litton Dri. DE21 46 D4
Lochinvar Clo. DE21 46 D3

Locko Ct. DE21 46 C2
Locko Rd. DE21 46 C2
Lodge La. DE21 46 C3
Longley La. DE21 46 B1
Lousie Greaves La.
  DE21 46 C2
Ludlow Clo. DE21 46 D3
Maine Dri. DE21 46 A1
Manor Park. DE72 47 E6
Manor Rd. DE72 47 E6
Marina Dri. DE21 46 C2
Maryland Rd. DE21 46 A1
Maylands. DE72 47 F6
Meadow Clo. DE21 46 C4
Mear Dri. DE72 47 F6
Meath Av. DE21 46 A3
Megaloughton La.
  DE21 46 A4
Merchant Av. DE21 46 B3
Mercian Mews. DE21 46 B3
Michigan Clo. DE21 46 B3
Mill Clo,
  Borrowash. DE72 47 F6
Mill Clo,
  Spondon. DE21 46 C3
Mill Row. DE21 46 C2
Milldale Rd. DE21 46 D4
Monsal Dri. DE21 46 D4
Moor End. DE21 46 D2
Moor La. DE72 47 F1
Moor St. DE21 46 C3
Moult Av. DE21 46 C3
New St. DE72 47 G3
Newbold Av. DE72 47 G6
Newhaven Rd. DE21 46 A2
Nicholas Clo. DE21 46 D2
Nottingham Rd,
  Borrowash. DE72 47 F6
Nottingham Rd,
  Spondon. DE21 46 C4
Nursery Clo. DE72 47 F5
Oak Clo. DE72 47 G2
Oak Tree Clo. DE72 47 G6
Oakridge. DE21 46 A1
Orchard Clo. DE21 47 F4
Orchard Ct. DE21 46 D2
Oregon Way. DE21 46 A1
Ormskirk Rise. DE21 46 D3
Oxford St. DE21 46 C3
Pamelas Clo. DE21 47 E2
Pares Way. DE72 47 F4
Park Leys Ct. DE21 46 D4
Park Rd. DE21 46 B3
Parkside Rd. DE21 46 A2
Paterson Av. DE21 46 A2
Peveril Av. DE21 47 G5
Pheasant Field Dri.
  DE21 47 E1
Pine Clo. DE21 46 A3
Pollards Oaks. DE72 47 F6
Poplar Av. DE21 46 C3
Potter St. DE21 46 C3
Priestland Av. DE21 46 B3
Princess Dri. DE21 47 E5
Priors Barn. DE72 47 G5
Priorway Av. DE72 47 G5
*Priorway Gdns,
  Priorway Av. DE72 47 G6
Quillings Way. DE72 47 G6
Rannoch Clo. DE21 46 D3
Raynesway. DE21 46 A4
Reader St. DE21 46 C2
Redstart Clo. DE21 46 D1
Robins Cross. DE72 47 F6
Roman Way. DE72 47 F6
Roosevelt Av. DE21 46 A1
Rose Av. DE72 47 G5
Rowan Clo. DE21 46 A3
Royal Clo. DE21 47 F6
Royal Hill Rd. DE21 46 B2
Rudyard Av. DE21 46 C2
Rutland Av. DE21 47 G5
Ryal Clo. DE72 47 G2
St Johns Av. DE21 46 A3
St Johns Clo. DE21 46 A3
St Stephens Clo. DE72 47 F6
St Werburghs Vw.
  DE21 46 B3
Sancroft Clo. DE21 46 C2
Sanderson Rd. DE21 46 A2
Sandringham Dri.
  DE21 46 D3
Shacklecross Clo.
  DE72 47 G6

Shannon Sq. DE21 46 A3
Sherwood Av. DE72 47 G5
Silverhill Rd. DE21 46 C4
Silvey Gro. DE21 46 C4
Sitwell Clo. DE21 46 C3
Sitwell St. DE21 46 C3
South Av. DE21 46 C3
Springfield Rd. DE21 46 A2
Station Rd,
  Borrowash. DE72 47 E6
Station Rd,
  Spondon. DE21 46 B4
Stewart Clo. DE21 46 D2
Stone Clo. DE21 46 C2
Stoney Cross. DE21 46 C4
Stoney La. DE21 46 D3
Strathaven Ct. DE21 46 C3
Sundew Clo. DE21 46 D3
Sunningdale Av. DE21 46 C2
Sunny Gro. DE21 46 A2
Sycamore Ct. DE21 46 C3
Tennessee Rd. DE21 46 A1
The Covert. DE21 46 D4
The Paddock. DE72 47 F3
The Pingle. DE72 47 F3
The Ridings. DE72 47 G2
The Settlement. DE72 47 F3
The Spinney. DE72 47 G6
Top Manor Clo. DE72 47 G3
Towle Clo. DE72 47 F6
Trent Rise. DE21 46 D3
Trenton Dri. DE21 46 A2
Trenton Grn. DE21 46 A1
Trevers Clo. DE21 46 D3
Ulswater Dri. DE21 46 C2
Valley Rd. DE21 46 D3
Vermont Dri. DE21 46 D4
Vernon Dri. DE21 46 D4
Victoria Av. DE72 47 F4
Vincent Av. DE21 46 D4
Washington Av. DE21 46 A1
Waterford Dri. DE21 46 C3
Weavers Dri. DE72 47 G6
Wensley Dri. DE21 46 C3
Werburgh Dri. DE21 46 C3
Wesley St. DE72 47 F2
West Rd. DE21 46 B2
Wey Acres. DE72 47 F6
Willowcroft Rd. DE21 46 C4
Windermere Dri. DE21 46 C2
Windmill Clo. DE72 47 G2
Windsor Clo. DE72 47 G6
Windsor Dri. DE21 46 C2
Wingerworth Pk Rd.
  DE21 46 C3
Winslow Gdns. DE21 46 A1
Wood Rd. DE21 47 E2
Woodland Av. DE72 47 G5
Woodwards Clo. DE72 47 G6
Yew Tree Av. DE72 47 G3

STAVELEY

Adelphi Way. S43 49 B5
Barlow Rd. S43 49 A3
Barnfield Clo. S43 49 A3
*Barnfield Walk,
  Barnfield Rd. S43 49 A3
Barrow St. S43 49 B3
Bellhouse La. S43 49 C2
Belmont Dri. S43 49 C2
Bent La. S43 49 C2
Bird St. S43 49 C2
Boundary Clo. S43 49 C2
Bridle Rd. S43 49 D3
Brierley Clo. S43 49 B3
Brindley Way. S43 49 B3
Calver Cres. S43 49 A5
Carpenter Av. S43 49 D2
Cavendish St. S43 49 A4
Cemetery La. S43 49 B4
Chatsworth St. S43 49 A5
Chesterfield Rd. S43 49 A4
Church St. S43 49 B3
College Av. S43 49 C5
Cottage Clo. S43 49 C5
Cranleigh Rd. S43 49 D2
Crompton Rd. S43 49 B3
Darley Clo. S43 49 B3
Deepdale Clo. S43 49 B1
Devonshire Clo. S43 49 B3

Devonshire St. S43 49 B3
Duke St. S43 49 B3
Eckington Rd. S43 49 B3
Elton Vw. S43 49 A5
Erin Rd. S43 49 B4
Fan Rd. S43 49 B4
Farndale Rd. S43 49 B1
Fern Av. S43 49 A5
Franklyn Dri. S43 49 B1
Frecheville St. S43 49 A4
*Gratton Ct,
  Eckington Rd. S43 49 B2
Griffen Clo. S43 49 B4
Haddon Pl. S43 49 B5
Hall La. S43 49 A1
Hartington View. S43 49 B1
Hassop Rd. S43 49 B2
Hayfield Clo. S43 49 B2
Hayford Way. S43 49 B4
High St. S43 49 B3
Hillcrest Gro. S43 49 B1
Howden Clo. S43 49 B1
Huntsman Rd. S43 49 A4
Immingham Gro. S43 49 A4
INDUSTRIAL ESTATES:
  Speedwell
  Ind Est. S43 49 B3
Inkersall Rd. S43 49 A6
Ireland Clo. S43 49 B3
Ireland St. S43 49 B3
*Leander Ct,
  Lowgates. S43 49 B2
Lime Av. S43 49 A3
Longshaw Clo. S43 49 A5
Lowfields. S43 49 C3
Lowgates. S43 49 B2
*Mallard Ct,
  Lowgates. S43 49 B2
Market Pl. S43 49 A3
Market St. S43 49 A3
Markham Cres. S43 49 B3
Marshfield Gro. S43 49 C3
Meadows Dri. S43 49 B4
Middlecroft Rd. S43 49 A5
Mill Grn. S43 49 A3
Milton Pl. S43 49 C3
Molineax Av. S43 49 A4
Moor View Rd. S43 49 C2
Netherfield Clo. S43 49 C2
Netherthorpe. S43 49 C3
Netherthorpe Clo. S43 49 C3
Netherthorpe Rd. S43 49 B3
Overton Clo. S43 49 B2
Poolsbrook Av. S43 49 C5
Poolsbrook Cres. S43 49 C5
Poolsbrook Sq. S43 49 C5
Poolsbrook Vw. S43 49 C5
Porter St. S43 49 B3
Pullman Clo. S43 49 C2
Ralph Rd. S43 49 C3
Rectory Rd. S43 49 B3
St Johns Pl. S43 49 A4
St Musard Pl. S43 49 A4
Staveley Rd. S43 49 C5
Stephenson Rd. S43 49 B4
Telford Cres. S43 49 B3
The Grove. S43 49 C5
Tollbridge Rd. S43 49 D2
Tudor St. S43 49 B3
Victoria Av. S43 49 C2
Warsop Rd. S43 49 C2
Wateringbury Gro. S43 49 B3
West Vw. S43 49 A4
Wharf La. S43 49 C2
White Rd. S43 49 C2
Whitehead St. S43 49 C3

SWADLINCOTE

Abbotts Clo. DE11 50 C2
Abbotts Rd. DE11 50 C2
Acacia. DE11 50 D1
Albert Rd. DE11 50 C6
Albion St. DE11 51 G6
Alexandra Rd. DE11 50 D4
Allison Rd. DE11 50 D4
Alma Rd. DE11 50 A2
Almond Gro. DE11 50 B3
Amberwood. DE11 50 B3
Anderby Gdns. DE11 50 B3
Appleton Clo. DE11 50 B2
Ascott Dri. DE11 50 C1

Ashby Rd. DE11 51 H6
Ashleigh Av. DE11 50 A2
Ashover Rd. DE11 50 A3
Ashtree Clo. DE11 50 B1
Audens Way. DE11 51 E2
Avon Clo. DE11 50 C2
Baker St. DE11 50 D5
Bakewell Grn. DE11 50 A3
Baltimore Clo. DE11 50 C1
Bank Pass. DE11 50 D4
Bardolph Clo. DE11 50 B5
Beards Rd. DE11 50 C2
Beech Gro. DE11 50 B1
Belfield Rd. DE11 50 D3
Belmont St. DE11 50 D4
Belvedere Rd. DE11 51 G5
Belvoir Cres. DE11 50 C2
Beresford Dale. DE11 50 A6
Bernard St. DE11 51 F5
Birch Av. DE11 50 B1
Blacksmiths La. DE11 51 G5
Boardman Rd. DE11 50 A5
Brair Clo. DE11 50 A3
Bretby Rd. DE11 50 A1
Bretby Vw. DE11 51 H4
Bridge Clo. DE11 50 D6
Bridge St. DE11 50 D6
Brook St,
  Newhall. DE11 50 A2
Brook St,
  Swadlincote. DE11 50 C5
Brookdale Rd. DE11 51 H4
Browning Rd. DE11 51 E2
Buckley Clo. DE11 51 H6
Burton Rd. DE11 50 D1
Butt La. DE11 51 H6
Buxton Clo. DE11 50 C1
Byron Rd. DE11 50 D2
Cadeleyhill Rd. DE11 50 A5
Cambrian Way. DE11 50 C5
Campion Rd. DE11 51 G4
Canner Clo. DE11 51 H6
Cavendish Clo. DE11 50 C1
Cecil Rd. DE11 50 B2
Cedar Gro. DE11 50 B1
Celandine Clo. DE11 51 G4
Chapel St,
  Newhall. DE11 50 B2
Chapel St,
  Woodville. DE11 51 G6
Charles St. DE11 50 C6
Charleston Clo. DE11 50 C1
Chatsworth Rd. DE11 50 C1
Cherrytree Clo. DE11 50 B2
Chester Gdns. DE11 50 D6
Chesterfield Av. DE11 50 A2
Chestnut Av. DE11 50 C1
Chestnut Grn. DE11 50 D5
Cheviot Clo. DE11 50 C5
Chiltern Rd. DE11 50 B5
Church Av. DE11 50 D5
Church Rd. DE11 50 C2
Church St,
  Newhall. DE11 50 B1
Church St,
  Swadlincote. DE11 50 C2
Civic Way. DE11 51 E4
Clamp Dri. DE11 50 C5
ClaymarDri. DE11 50 C1
Cleveland Clo. DE11 50 C5
Clifton Clo. DE11 50 B5
Clover Dale. DE11 50 D1
Common Rd. DE11 50 D6
Common Side. DE11 50 D6
Coppice Side. DE11 50 D5
Copse Rise. DE11 50 C1
Coronation St. DE11 50 C3
Cotswold Clo. DE11 50 C5
Cottage Clo. DE11 50 B1
Court St. DE11 51 F4
Coventry Clo. DE11 51 E2
Craythorne Clo. DE11 50 B1
Crich Way. DE11 50 A3
Dalefield Dri. DE11 50 D5
Dalston Rd. DE11 50 C4
Darklands Rd. DE11 50 C4
Darley Dale. DE11 50 A6
Davis Rd. DE11 50 C3
Derby Rd. DE11 51 E4
Dickens Dri. DE11 51 E2
Dominion Rd. DE11 50 D3
Dove Clo. DE11 51 G4
Drayton St. DE11 50 D4

Dundee Rd. DE11 51 E2
Dunnsmoor La. DE11 51 F1
Dunsmore Way. DE11 51 F2
Durham Rd. DE11 51 F2
Eastfield Rd. DE11 50 D2
Edgecote Dri. DE11 50 C1
Edward St. DE11 51 H4
Elmsdale Rd. DE11 51 H4
Elmsleigh Clo. DE11 50 C1
Elmsleigh Dri. DE11 50 C1
Elmsleigh Grn. DE11 50 D2
Ely Clo. DE11 51 E1
Ernest Hall Way. DE11 50 D4
Eureka Rd. DE11 51 E3
Exeter Clo. DE11 51 F2
Fabis Clo. DE11 50 B5
Fairfield Cres. DE11 50 A3
Fairfield Ter. DE11 51 G5
Falcon Way. DE11 51 G4
Farm Side. DE11 50 B3
Field Way. DE11 50 B2
Finch Clo. DE11 51 H5
Forman Clo. DE11 50 D3
Foster Rd. DE11 51 G6
Frederick St. DE11 51 F5
George St. DE11 50 B6
Glebe St. DE11 50 C5
George Holmes Way.
  DE11 50 B4
Goseley Av. DE11 51 H3
Goseley Cres. DE11 51 H4
Granville Ct. DE11 51 E4
Granville St. DE11 51 F5
Gregson Clo. DE11 50 D3
Gresley Wood Rd.
  DE11 50 B5
Gresley Woodlands.
  DE11 50 B6
Grove St. DE11 50 D4
Guildford Av. DE11 51 F2
Hall Farm Clo. DE11 51 E4
Hall Farm Rd. DE11 51 E4
Hall St. DE11 50 C6
Hamilton Dri. DE11 51 E3
Hamilton Gro. DE11 51 E3
Handsacre Clo. DE11 50 B5
Harebell Clo. DE11 51 G4
Harrow Rd. DE11 50 D1
Hartshill Rd. DE11 51 H4
Hartshorne Rd. DE11 51 G5
Harvest Hill. DE11 50 C1
Hastings Rd. DE11 50 D5
Hawthorn Rise. DE11 50 B1
Hay Wain La. DE11 50 C1
Hazel Clo. DE11 50 B3
Hearthcote Rd. DE11 50 A5
Hedge Gro. DE11 50 C1
Hereford Cres. DE11 51 E2
Hermitage Park Way.
  DE11 50 C1
Heron Dri. DE11 51 H4
Higgins Rd. DE11 50 A1
High St,
  Newhall. DE11 50 B1
High St,
  Swadlincote. DE11 50 D4
High St,
  Woodville. DE11 51 G5
Highfield Rd. DE11 50 D5
Highfield St. DE11 50 C2
Hill St, Newhall. DE11 50 B1
Hill St,
  Swadlincote. DE11 51 E4
Holly Ct. DE11 51 H6
Hollybank Clo. DE11 50 C1
Honeysuckle Clo. DE11 50 B2
Howden Clo. DE11 50 B5
INDUSTRIAL ESTATES:
  Boardmans Ind Est.
  DE11 50 A5
  George Holmes
  Business Pk. DE11 50 B4
  Granville Ind Est.
  DE11 51 E5
  Hearthcote Rd
  Ind Est. DE11 50 C4
Ingleby Clo. DE11 50 B5
James St. DE11 51 E2
John St,
  Newhall. DE11 50 A2
John St,
  Swadlincote. DE11 50 D3
John St,
  Woodville. DE11 51 E6

Kay Dri. DE11 50 B2
Keats Dri. DE11 50 D2
Kestrel Clo. DE11 51 G5
Kilburn Way. DE11 50 B2
Kiln Way. DE11 51 E5
Kinder Av. DE11 50 C2
Kingfisher Av. DE11 51 H4
Kings Rd. DE11 50 B1
Laburnham Rd. DE11 50 B1
Ladyfields. DE11 51 E2
Lansdowne Rd. DE11 50 C4
Lathkill Dale. DE11 50 B5
*Lawns Dri,
  Edgecote Dri. DE11 50 C1
Leawood Rd. DE11 51 E1
Lichfield Av. DE11 51 F2
Lime Tree Av. DE11 51 E3
Lincoln Way. DE11 51 F3
Longlands Rd. DE11 51 E1
Main St, Church
  Gresley. DE11 51 E6
Main St,
  Newhall. DE11 50 A2
Malmesbury Av. DE11 51 E2
Manton Clo. DE11 50 B2
Maple Rd. DE11 50 C2
Market St, Church
  Gresley. DE11 50 D6
Market St,
  Swadlincote. DE11 50 D4
Maryland Clo. DE11 50 C1
Masefield Av. DE11 51 E2
Matsyard Footpath.
  DE11 50 B1
Mayfair. DE11 50 A2
Maypole Hill. DE11 50 B2
Meadow La. DE11 50 B2
Meadow View Rd.
  DE11 50 A3
Meadow Way. DE11 50 B2
Merlin Way. DE11 51 G5
Mickleton Clo. DE11 50 D6
Midland Rd. DE11 50 D4
Midway Rd. DE11 51 E2
Mill Clo. DE11 51 E3
Millfield Croft. DE11 50 C1
Millfield St. DE11 51 H5
Milton Way. DE11 51 E2
Moat St. DE11 50 C6
Moira Rd. DE11 51 F6
Mount Rd. DE11 51 H4
Nelson St. DE11 50 D3
New Rd,
  Newhall. DE11 50 A2
New Rd,
  Woodville. DE11 51 G6
New St. DE11 50 D6
Newhall Rd. DE11 50 D3
Newlands Clo. DE11 50 C6
*Newton Park Pl,
  Edgecote Dri. DE11 50 C1
Nightingale Dri. DE11 51 G5
North St. DE11 50 D3
Nursery Clo. DE11 50 D2
Oak St. DE11 50 C6
Oakleigh Av. DE11 50 A2
Occupation La. DE11 51 F6
Old Hall Gdns. DE11 50 B6
Oldfield Dri. DE11 50 D3
Orchard St. DE11 50 B1
Oversetts Ct. DE11 50 A2
Oversetts Rd. DE11 50 A2
Oxford St. DE11 50 C6
Park Ct. DE11 50 D3
Park Rd. DE11 50 D5
Park St. DE11 50 B1
Parliament St. DE11 50 A2
Partridge Dri. DE11 51 G5
Pear Tree Av. DE11 50 B1
Pennine Way. DE11 50 C5
Pine Gro. DE11 50 B2
Pingle Rd. DE11 50 B2
Plover Av. DE11 51 G5
Plummer Rd. DE11 50 B2
Pool St. DE11 51 E5
Poplar Av. DE11 50 C1
Prestwood Park Dri.
  DE11 51 E2
Primrose Mdw. DE11 50 D1
Princess Clo. DE11 51 G5
Priory Clo. DE11 50 C2
Queens Dri. DE11 50 C2
Rambler Clo. DE11 50 C2

Randall Clo. DE11 50 D4
Redhill Lodge Rd. DE11 50 C1
Regent St. DE11 50 C6
Renshaw Dri. DE11 50 A2
Repton Rd. DE11 51 G1
Rest Haven. DE11 50 D3
Rink Dri. DE11 50 D4
Robian Way. DE11 50 C4
Robin Hood Pl. DE11 50 D6
Robinson Rd. DE11 50 B2
Rockcliffe Clo. DE11 50 D6
Rose Hill. DE11 51 F5
Rose Tree La. DE11 50 A1
Rose Valley. DE11 50 B2
Rosecroft Gdns. DE11 50 D5
Roseleigh Cres. DE11 50 B2
Rowley Clo. DE11 50 C1
Russell St. DE11 51 E4
Ruston Clo. DE11 50 C4
St Catherines Rd. DE11 50 B2
St Edwards Ct. DE11 50 A3
St Johns Dri. DE11 50 A2
St Stephens Clo. DE11 51 G5
Salisbury Dri. DE11 51 F3
Sandcliffe Park. DE11 51 E1
Sandcliffe Rd. DE11 51 E2
Sandcroft Clo. DE11 51 F3
School St. DE11 50 C6
Shakespeare Clo. DE11 50 D2
Sharpeswood Manor. DE11 51 G4
Shelley Rd. DE11 50 D2
Smallthorn Pl. DE11 51 G6
Solney Clo. DE11 50 B5
Sorrel Dri. DE11 51 G4
South Dri. DE11 50 B2
South St. DE11 51 H6
Springfield Clo. DE11 50 D1
Springfield Rd. DE11 50 D3
Springwood Farm Rd. DE11 50 C1
Stanhope Rd. DE11 50 C4
Stanley Clo. DE11 51 G5
Stanley St. DE11 51 E4
Station Rd. DE11 51 H5
Stoneydale Clo. DE11 50 B3
Sun St. DE11 51 G6
Sunnyside. DE11 50 A1
Swadlincote La. DE11 50 A6
Swadlincote Rd. DE11 51 F5
Swallow Rd. DE11 51 G5
Swift Clo. DE11 51 G5
Sycamore Av. DE11 50 B1
Talbot St. DE11 50 C6
Tennyson Av. DE11 50 D2
Tern Av. DE11 51 G5
The Burrows. DE11 50 B2
The Castle Mews. DE11 50 C1
The City. DE11 51 H6
The Crescent. DE11 50 A2
The Croft. DE11 50 A2
The Fairway. DE11 50 A2
The Gables. DE11 50 A2
The Holdings. DE11 50 C6
The Leys. DE11 50 A2
The Paddocks. DE11 50 B3
The Pastures. DE11 50 B3
The Rise. DE11 50 A3
The Sandlands. DE11 51 E1
The Shrubbery. DE11 51 H6
The Tythe. DE11 50 D1
Thorn St. DE11 51 H6
Thorn Tree La. DE11 50 B1
Thorpe Downs Rd. DE11 50 D6
Tideswell Grn. DE11 50 A3
Top Mdw. DE11 50 D1
Toulmin Dri. DE11 50 C4
Tower Rd. DE11 51 H2
Trinity Gro. DE11 50 D5
Truro Clo. DE11 51 G2
Tudor Ho Mews. DE11 50 B1
Tudor Way. DE11 50 C2
Twyford Clo. DE11 50 B5
Union Rd. DE11 50 C2
Vale Rd, Upper Midway. DE11 50 C2
Vale Rd, Woodville. DE11 51 H5
Valley Rise. DE11 50 B1
Vicarage Gdns. DE11 51 E4

Vicarage Rd, Swadlincote. DE11 51 E4
Vicarage Rd, Woodville. DE11 51 G6
Victoria Villas. DE11 50 C2
Walton Clo. DE11 50 C5
Walnut Clo. DE11 50 B3
Warwick Clo. DE11 51 F2
Waterloo Pl. DE11 50 A4
Wellwood Rd. DE11 50 B2
West St. DE11 50 D4
Westacres Dri. DE11 50 A5
Westfield Rd. DE11 50 D2
Weston St. DE11 50 D5
Westwood Park. DE11 50 B2
Wheatlands. DE11 50 C1
Wideshaft. DE11 51 E3
William Nadins Way. DE11 50 A4
Willow Clo. DE11 50 D4
Willow Rise. DE11 50 B1
Wilmot Rd. DE11 50 C4
Winchester Dri. DE11 51 F2
Windmill St. DE11 50 C6
Windsor Clo. DE11 50 C1
Winster Grn. DE11 50 A3
Wolfscote Dale. DE11 50 B6
Wood La. DE11 50 B1
Wood St. DE11 50 C5
Woodfield Dri. DE11 50 D2
Woodhouse St. DE11 51 E5
Woodview Rd. DE11 50 A3
Woodville Rd. DE11 51 H4
Woodwards Pl. DE11 50 D5
Wordsworth Av. DE11 51 E2
Wren Clo. DE11 51 G4
Wye Dale. DE11 50 A6
Yewtree Rd. DE11 50 B1
York Clo. DE11 51 E2
York Rd. DE11 50 C6

TIBSHELF

Addison St. DE55 52 D2
Alfreton Rd. DE55 52 B4
Arran Ct. DE55 52 C3
Babbington St. DE55 52 D3
Back La. DE55 52 C3
Bank Clo. DE55 52 C4
Boundary Gdns. DE55 52 D3
Brooke St. DE55 52 D2
Chatsworth St. DE55 52 D3
Chesterfield Rd. DE55 52 D1
Chestnut Gro. DE55 52 C4
Church La. DE55 52 C2
Derwent Dri. DE55 52 C3
Doe Hill La. DE55 52 A4
Fox Croft. DE55 52 C4
Foxpark View. DE55 52 B4
Haddon St. DE55 52 D2
Hardwick St. DE55 52 D2
Harrison La. DE55 52 C3
Hawthorne Av. DE55 52 E1
Heathfield Gdns. DE55 52 D2
High St. DE55 52 C3
Iona Clo. DE55 52 C3
Kedleston Ct. DE55 52 E3
King St. DE55 52 D2
Lathkil Gro. DE55 52 C3
Lincoln Clo. DE55 52 D2
Lincoln St. DE55 52 D2
Little Fen. DE55 52 C4
Mansfield Rd. DE55 52 E2
Meadow Clo. DE55 52 E2
Monsal Cres. DE55 52 C3
Newton Rd. DE55 52 C3
Newtonwood La. DE55 52 E4
Pennine Clo. DE55 52 C3
Peveril Rd. DE55 52 C3
Pewit La. DE55 52 A3
Raven Av. DE55 52 C3
St Thomas Clo. DE55 52 C4
Saw Pit La. DE55 52 E4
Shetland Rd. DE55 52 C4
Sitwell Grange La. DE55 52 A1
Skye Clo. DE55 52 C3
Spa Croft. DE55 52 C4
Staffa Dri. DE55 52 C3
Station Rd. DE55 52 C3
Sunny Bank. DE55 52 C3
Tiree Clo. DE55 52 C3
Vicar La. DE55 52 D2

Waverley St. DE55 52 D2
West View. DE55 52 C3
Westwood La. DE55 52 C2
Wharf La. DE55 52 F2
Whettons La. DE55 52 C3
Winkpenny La. DE55 52 C3

TINTWISTLE/ HADFIELD

Albert St. SK14 53 C3
Arnfield La. SK14 53 C1
Arrowscroft Way. SK14 53 A3
Ashes La. SK13 53 D6
Ashfield Rd. SK14 53 B5
Bamford La. SK13 53 A6
Bank La. SK14 53 C1
Bank St. SK14 53 C3
Bankbottom. SK14 53 C2
Bankswood Clo. SK14 53 C4
Barley Croft. SK14 53 B4
Beatrix Dri. SK14 53 A4
Beechfield Rd. SK14 53 B5
Bidworth La. SK14 53 A6
Blenheim Clo. SK14 53 D3
*Bonsall Bank, Melandra Castle Rd. SK13 53 A6
*Bonsall Fold, Melandra Castle Rd. SK13 53 A6
*Bonsall Wk, Melandra Castle Rd. SK13 53 A6
Bracken Clo. SK14 53 A2
Brahma Edge Ct. SK14 53 C1
Brassington Cres. SK13 53 A6
Brickfield St. SK14 53 D3
Brookfield. SK13 53 B5
Brookside Clo. SK14 53 C4
Brosscroft. SK14 53 D2
Brosscroft Village. SK14 53 D2
Burnside. SK14 53 B4
Buxton Mews. SK13 53 A6
Buxton Ter. SK14 53 A2
*Calver Clo, Hathersage Cres. SK13 53 A6
*Calver Pl, Hathersage Cres. SK13 53 A6
Calver Mews. SK13 53 A6
Castle St. SK14 53 C4
Chapel La. SK14 53 B3
Chapel Walk. SK14 53 C3
Chapelbrow. SK14 53 D1
Chesham Clo. SK14 53 D3
Church St, Hadfield. SK14 53 C3
Church St, Tintwistle. SK14 53 C1
Combs Mews. SK14 53 A6
Conduit St. SK14 53 C1
Cottage La. SK14 53 B6
Creambank. SK14 53 C3
Cross St, Hadfield. SK14 53 C3
Cross St, Hollingworth. SK14 53 A4
Crossgate La. SK14 53 B1
Dinting La. SK13 53 D6
Dinting Rd. SK13 53 D6
Dinting Vale. SK13 53 B6
Earnshaw St. SK14 53 A4
Edale Cres. SK13 53 B6
Ellison Clo. SK14 53 A3
Elminger Av. SK14 53 D2
Etherow Way. SK14 53 B3
Evesham Dri. SK14 53 D3
Evesham Way. SK13 53 B5
Exam Mews. SK13 53 A6
Eyam La. SK13 53 A6
Fay Gdns. SK14 53 B4
*Fern Lea, Buxton Ter. SK14 53 A2
Fernlea Clo. SK14 53 B4
Fields Cres. SK14 53 A2
Fields Gro. SK14 53 A2
Gas St. SK14 53 C3
Gawsworth Clo. SK14 53 D3
Gladstone St. SK14 53 C4
Glossop Rd. SK13 53 B6
Goddard La. SK14 53 C3
Goddard St. SK14 53 C3
Grassmoor Cres. SK13 53 A6

Green La, Hadfield. SK14 53 B4
Green La, Hollingworth. SK14 53 A3
Greenfield St. SK14 53 D2
Grindleford Gro. SK13 53 A6
*Hadfields Av, Market St. SK14 53 A3
Hadfield Rd. SK14 53 B3
*Hadfields Av, Market St. SK14 53 A3
Hathersage Cres. SK13 53 A6
Hawthorne Bank. SK14 53 B4
Hawthorne Gro. SK14 53 A2
Heather Gro. SK14 53 A2
High Bank. SK14 53 C1
Higher Barn Rd. SK14 53 B4
Highfield Gdns. SK14 53 B4
Hillside Clo. SK14 53 B4
Hilltop Rd. SK13 53 D6
Hollins La. SK13 53 A6
Hollins Mews. SK13 53 A6
Holly Bank. SK14 53 A3
INDUSTRIAL ESTATES:
Dinting Lodge Ind Est. SK14 53 B5
Ivycroft. SK14 53 B4
John Dalton Rd. SK14 53 C3
John St. SK14 53 C4
Jones St. SK14 53 C2
*Junction St, Woolley La. SK14 53 C3
Kiln La. SK14 53 C3
King St. SK14 53 C2
Lake Side. SK14 53 D3
Lambgates. SK14 53 D3
Langley Ct. SK14 53 D3
Langsette La. SK13 53 A6
Lawn Fold. SK14 53 B4
Littlebrook Clo. SK14 53 C4
Litton Mews. SK13 53 B6
Lodge Bank. SK14 53 B4
Longnor Mews. SK13 53 A6
Lord St. SK14 53 A4
Lower Bank Clo. SK14 53 C5
Lower Barn Rd. SK14 53 B4
Maguire Av. SK14 53 D2
Malvern Rise. SK14 53 D3
Manchester Rd. SK14 53 A3
Market St. SK14 53 A3
Marlow St. SK14 53 D3
Marsden St. SK14 53 C3
Masons Gro. SK14 53 B4
Matthew Clo. SK14 53 B1
Meadow Bank. SK14 53 A2
*Meadowfield Ct, Shaw La. SK14 53 C5
Melandra Castle Rd. SK13 53 A6
Mersey Bank Rd. SK14 53 B3
*Millbrook, Manchester Rd. SK14 53 A2
*Moorfield Precinct, Moorfield Ter. SK14 53 A3
Moorfield St. SK14 53 A3
Moorfield Ter. SK14 53 A3
Moss St. SK14 53 C3
Mossbank Clo. SK14 53 B4
Mouselow Clo. SK14 53 C5
New Bank. SK14 53 C3
New Rd. SK14 53 C1
New Shaw La. SK14 53 A4
Newlands Dri. SK14 53 C4
North Brook Rd. SK14 53 B4
North Clo. SK14 53 B1
Oakfield Rd. SK14 53 C3
Old Hall Sq. SK14 53 C3
Old Rd. SK14 53 C1
Organ Way. SK14 53 B5
Osbourne Pl. SK14 53 C3
Padfield Main Rd. SK14 53 D2
Paradise St. SK14 53 D4
Park Rd. SK14 53 D4
Peacock Clo. SK14 53 B4
Peakdale Rd. SK13 53 B5
Pear Tree Clo. SK14 53 B4
Peter St. SK14 53 D2
Pinfold. SK14 53 B4
Platt St. SK14 53 D3
Potter Rd. SK14 53 A4
Printers Fold. SK14 53 A3
Printers Park. SK14 53 A3
Queen St. SK14 53 C4

Railway St. SK14 53 D3
Redfern Clo. SK14 53 D2
Rhodeswood Dri. SK14 53 D2
Riber Bank. SK13 53 A6
Riddings Rd. SK14 53 C3
Ridge Clo. SK14 53 B4
Ross Bank Rd. SK14 53 A3
Roundhill Clo. SK14 53 C5
Rowan Walk. SK14 53 B4
Rowsley Mews. SK13 53 B6
*Rowsley Wk, Melandra Castle Rd. SK14 53 A6
*St Andrews Ct, South Marlow St. SK14 53 D3
St Charles Clo. SK14 53 C3
Salisbury St. SK14 53 C3
Sandybank Clo. SK14 53 B4
Sexton St. SK14 53 C1
Shaw La. SK13 53 B5
Shawfield Rd. SK14 53 B5
Sheldon Mews. SK13 53 A6
South Clo. SK14 53 B1
South Marlow St. SK14 53 D3
Southbrook Clo. SK14 53 B4
Speedwell. SK14 53 C1
Spring Gdns. SK14 53 C3
Springbank. SK14 53 C3
Springfield Clo. SK14 53 B4
Springwater Dri. SK14 53 A4
Stanyforth St. SK14 53 C3
Station Rd. SK14 53 C3
Stiles Clo. SK14 53 B3
Stocks. SK14 53 D1
Stoneridge. SK14 53 C3
Sutton Way. SK14 53 D3
Tavern Rd. SK14 53 A4
Taylor St. SK14 53 A3
The Avenue. SK14 53 C4
The Boulevard. SK14 53 B4
The Carriage Dri. SK14 53 B3
The Courtyard. SK14 53 A3
The Croft. SK14 53 C2
The Cross. SK14 53 C3
The Grove. SK14 53 B4
The Lodge. SK14 53 C2
The Moorlands. SK14 53 D3
The Paddock, Hadfield. SK14 53 B3
The Paddock, Hollingworth. SK14 53 C3
The Rises. SK14 53 C3
The Rushes. SK14 53 B4
The Shaw. SK13 53 C5
The Sycamores. SK14 53 B5
Thorncliffe Rd. SK14 53 B4
Torside Vw. SK14 53 D2
Vale House Dri. SK14 53 D2
Victoria Av. SK14 53 D3
Walker St. SK14 53 C3
Water La. SK14 53 A3
Waterside. SK14 53 C2
Watkin Av. SK14 53 B4
Weatcroft. SK14 53 B4
Wesley St. SK14 53 C3
*Wessington Bank, Hathersage Cres. SK13 53 A6
*Wessington Mews, Hathersage Cres. SK13 53 A6
West Dri. SK14 53 B1
West St. SK14 53 C1
Wharncliffe Clo. SK14 53 B4
Wilmans Wk. SK14 53 D2
Winchester Mws. SK13 53 A6
Woodfield Clo. SK14 53 B4
Woodhead Rd. SK14 53 D1
Woodlands Clo. SK14 53 C1
Woolley Bridge. SK14 53 A4
Woolley Bridge Rd. SK14 53 A4
Woolley Clo. SK14 53 A4
Woolley La. SK14 53 A4
Woolley La. SK14 53 A2
Woolley Mill La. SK14 53 A1

WHALEY BRIDGE

Alder Rise. SK12 54 A3
Beech Rise. SK12 54 A6
Beech Clo. SK12 54 B4
Bings Rd. SK12 54 C4

Bingswood Rd. SK12 54 B4
Brookside. SK12 54 D3
Buxton Rd. SK12 54 B1
Canal St. SK12 54 B3
Chapel Rd. SK12 54 B5
Church Bank. SK12 54 B4
Craig Dri. SK12 54 C5
Crescent Dri. SK12 54 B1
Cromford Ct. SK12 54 B6
Eccles Clo. SK12 54 A3
Eccles Rd. SK12 54 C6
Elnor Av. SK12 54 C6
Elnor La. SK12 54 C6
Forge Rd. SK12 54 B4
George St. SK12 54 C3
Goyt Rd. SK12 54 B5
Hill Dri. SK12 54 A3
Hill Top Rise. SK12 54 A3
Hill View. SK12 54 A3
Hockerley Av. SK12 54 A3
Hockerley Clo. SK12 54 B3
Hockerley La. SK12 54 B3
INDUSTRIAL ESTATES:
 Bingswood
 Ind Est. SK12 54 C3
Jodrell Mdw. SK12 54 B3
Jodrell Rd. SK12 54 B3
Lanehead Rd. SK12 54 A6
Linglongs Av. SK12 54 A6
Linglongs Rd. SK12 54 A6
Low Meadow. SK12 54 A3
Lower Macclesfield Rd.
 SK12 54 B5
Macclesfield Rd. SK12 54 A5
Manor Rd. SK12 54 B6

Market St. SK12 54 B4
Meadow Clo. SK12 54 A3
Meadowfield. SK12 54 A3
Meadowside. SK12 54 A3
Mereside Gdns. SK12 54 A5
Mevril Rd. SK12 54 B6
New Horwich Rd. SK12 54 B4
New Rd,
 Bridgemont. SK12 54 B1
New Rd,
 Horwich End. SK12 54 B5
Old Rd. SK12 54 B4
Orchard Av. SK12 54 B4
Orchard Rd. SK12 54 B4
Paddock La. SK12 54 C6
Reddish Av. SK12 54 A5
Reddish La. SK12 54 A5
Reddish Rd. SK12 54 B5
Reservoir Rd. SK12 54 A4
Ringstone Way. SK12 54 A2
Rock Bank. SK12 54 B5
Shallcross Mill Rd.
 SK12 54 C6
Silk Hill. SK12 54 D3
Start La. SK12 54 A4
The Coppice. SK12 54 C6
The Paddock. SK12 54 C5
The Rise. SK12 54 A6
Toddbrook Clo. SK12 54 A5
Vaughan Rd. SK12 54 B6
Waterfoot La. SK12 54 A5
Western La. SK12 54 D3
Whaley Rd. SK12 54 A3
Wharf St. SK12 54 B4

Williamson Cres. SK12 54 B3
Williamson Rd. SK12 54 B3
Woodbrook. SK12 54 B3
Yeardsley Grn. SK12 54 A3

WIRKSWORTH

Adam Bede Cres. DE4 55 B6
Arkwright St. DE4 55 B5
Barmote Croft. DE4 55 B4
Blind La. DE4 55 B4
Bournebrook Av. DE4 55 B6
Bowling Green La. DE4 55 B4
Breamfield La. DE4 55 D5
Brickfields Clo. DE4 55 C1
Brooklands Av. DE4 55 B5
Canterbury Rd. DE4 55 B5
Canterbury Ter. DE4 55 B5
Cat Hill. DE4 55 B5
Cavendish Cotts. DE4 55 B3
Cemetery La. DE4 55 B3
Chapel La. DE4 55 B4
Church St. DE4 55 B4
Cinder La. DE4 55 A6
Coldwell St. DE4 55 B4
Copse Clo. DE4 55 A5
Crabtree Clo. DE4 55 A5
Cromford Hill. DE4 55 B1
Cromford Rd. DE4 55 B3
Crown Yard. DE4 55 B4
Dark La. DE4 55 B1
Derby Rd. DE4 55 B6
Ellesbourne Clo. DE4 55 B5

Gorsey Bank. DE4 55 C6
Green Hill. DE4 55 A3
Greenway Croft. DE4 55 B4
Griggs Gdns. DE4 55 C5
Hammonds Ct. DE4 55 B4
Harrison Dri. DE4 55 B4
Hey La. DE4 55 D6
Hopton Ridge. DE4 55 A3
Ian Av. DE4 55 B5
Jubilee Ct. DE4 55 A6
King Edward St. DE4 55 C4
King George St. DE4 55 B5
Kingsfield Rd. DE4 55 A6
Ladyflatts Rd. DE4 55 A5
Little Bolehill. DE4 55 C2
Main St. DE4 55 B1
Malthouse Clo. DE4 55 B1
Market Pl. DE4 55 B4
Memorial Croft. DE4 55 C2
Middleton Rd. DE4 55 A2
Millers Grn. DE4 55 A6
Mount Ford Av. DE4 55 B5
Nan Gells Hill. DE4 55 C2
Nether Gdns. DE4 55 B4
New Rd. DE4 55 C2
Norbreck La. DE4 55 A3
North End. DE4 55 B4
Nursery Croft. DE4 55 A6
Oakerthorpe Rd. DE4 55 C1
Old La. DE4 55 B2
Pillar Butts. DE4 55 B5
Pittywood Rd. DE4 55 A5
Porter La. DE4 55 A1
Pratthall La. DE4 55 C6
Ravenstor Rd. DE4 55 B2

Recreation Rd. DE4 55 A5
St Helens La. DE4 55 C5
St Johns St. DE4 55 B4
St Marys Gate. DE4 55 B4
Slater Cres. DE4 55 B6
Snowfield Vw. DE4 55 A6
Sough La,
 Bolehill. DE4 55 D2
Sough La,
 Wirksworth. DE4 55 B3
South View. DE4 55 B3
Stafford Cres. DE4 55 A5
Steeple Grange. DE4 55 B2
Stoney Hill. DE4 55 C3
Summer Dri. DE4 55 A5
Summer La. DE4 55 A5
The Causeway. DE4 55 B4
The Dale. DE4 55 A3
The Lanes. DE4 55 C2
Thorn Tree Cotts. DE4 55 B3
Vernon Cotts. DE4 55 B3
Warmbrook. DE4 55 B5
Wash Green. DE4 55 C4
Water La. DE4 55 B5
West End. DE4 55 B4
Willowbath La. DE4 55 B5
Wirksworth Hall Gdns.
 DE4 55 B4
Wood St. DE4 55 B5
Woodlands. DE4 55 A5
Yokecliffe Av. DE4 55 A5
Yokecliffe Cres. DE4 55 A5
Yokecliffe Dri. DE4 55 A5
Yokecliffe Hill. DE4 55 A5

ESTATE PUBLICATIONS

STREET ATLASES

ALFRETON, BELPER, RIPLEY
ASHFORD, TENTERDEN
BANGOR, CAERNARFON
BARNSTAPLE, ILFRACOMBE
BASILDON, BILLERICAY
BASINGSTOKE, ANDOVER
BATH, BRADFORD-ON-AVON
BEDFORD
BOURNEMOUTH, POOLE, CHRISTCHURCH
BRENTWOOD
BRIGHTON, LEWES, NEWHAVEN, SEAFORD
BRISTOL
BROMLEY (London Borough)
BURTON-ON-TRENT
BURY ST. EDMUNDS
CAMBRIDGE
CARDIFF
CHELMSFORD, BRAINTREE, MALDON, WITHAM
CHESTER
CHESTERFIELD
CHICHESTER, BOGNOR REGIS
COATBRIDGE, AIRDRIE
COLCHESTER, CLACTON
CONNAH'S QUAY
CORBY, KETTERING
CRAWLEY & MID SUSSEX
CREWE
DERBY, HEANOR, CASTLE DONINGTON
EASTBOURNE
EDINBURGH, MUSSELBURGH
EXETER, EXMOUTH
FALKIRK, GRANGEMOUTH
FAREHAM, GOSPORT
FOLKESTONE, DOVER, DEAL
GLASGOW & PAISLEY
GLOUCESTER, CHELTENHAM
GRAVESEND, DARTFORD
GRAYS, THURROCK
GRIMSBY, CLEETHORPES
GUILDFORD, WOKING
HAMILTON, MOTHERWELL
HARLOW, BISHOPS STORTFORD
HASTINGS
HERTFORD, HODDESDON
HIGH WYCOMBE
HUNTINGDON, ST. NEOTS
IPSWICH, FELIXSTOWE
ISLE OF WIGHT TOWNS
KINGSTON-UPON-HULL
LANCASTER, MORECAMBE
LEICESTER, LOUGHBOROUGH
LINCOLN
LLANDUDNO, COLWYN BAY
LUTON, DUNSTABLE
MAIDSTONE
MANSFIELD
MEDWAY, GILLINGHAM
MILTON KEYNES
NEW FOREST TOWNS
NEWPORT, CHEPSTOW
NEWTOWN, WELSHPOOL
NORTHAMPTON
NORWICH
NOTTINGHAM, EASTWOOD, HUCKNALL, ILKESTON
OXFORD, ABINGDON
PETERBOROUGH
PLYMOUTH, IVYBRIDGE, SALTASH, TORPOINT
PORTSMOUTH, HAVANT
READING
REIGATE, BANSTEAD, LEATHERHEAD, DORKING
RHYL, PRESTATYN
ST. ALBANS, WELWYN, HATFIELD
SALISBURY, AMESBURY, WILTON
SCUNTHORPE
SEVENOAKS
SHREWSBURY
SITTINGBOURNE, FAVERSHAM
SLOUGH, MAIDENHEAD
SOUTHAMPTON, EASTLEIGH
SOUTHEND-ON-SEA
STAFFORD
STEVENAGE, HITCHIN
STIRLING
STOKE ON TRENT
STROUD, NAILSWORTH
SWANSEA, NEATH
SWINDON, CHIPPENHAM
TAUNTON, BRIDGWATER
TELFORD
THANET, CANTERBURY, HERNE BAY, WHITSTABLE
TORBAY
TRURO & FALMOUTH
TUNBRIDGE WELLS, TONBRIDGE, CROWBOROUGH
WATFORD, HEMEL HEMPSTEAD
WEALDEN TOWNS
WELLINGBOROUGH
WESTON-SUPER-MARE
WEYMOUTH, DORCHESTER
WINCHESTER, NEW ALRESFORD
WORTHING, LITTLEHAMPTON, ARUNDEL
WREXHAM

LEISURE MAPS

SOUTH EAST ENGLAND (1:200,000)
KENT & EAST SUSSEX (1:150,000)
SUSSEX & SURREY (1:150,000)
SOUTHERN ENGLAND (1:200,000)
ISLE OF WIGHT (1:50,000)
WESSEX (1:200,000)
DEVON & CORNWALL (1:200,000)
CORNWALL (1:180,000)
DEVON (1:200,000)
DARTMOOR & SOUTH DEVON COAST (1:100,000)
EXMOOR & NORTH DEVON COAST (1:100,000)
GREATER LONDON M25 (1:80,000)
EAST ANGLIA (1:200,000)
CHILTERNS & THAMES VALLEY (1:200,000)
THE COTSWOLDS (1:110,000)
COTSWOLDS & WYEDEAN (1:200,000)
WALES (1:250,000)
CYMRU (1;250,000)
THE SHIRES OF MIDDLE ENGLAND (1:250,000)
STAFFORDSHIRE & SHROPSHIRE (1:200,000)
PEAK DISTRICT (1:100,000)
SNOWDONIA (1:125,000)
YORKSHIRE (1:200,000)
YORKSHIRE DALES (1:125,000)
NORTH YORKSHIRE MOORS (1:125,000)
NORTH WEST ENGLAND (1:200,000)
ISLE OF MAN (1:60,000)
NORTH PENNINES & LAKES (1:200,000)
LAKE DISTRICT (1:75,000)
BORDERS OF ENGLAND & SCOTLAND (1:200,000)
BURNS COUNTRY (1:200,000)
HEART OF SCOTLAND (1:200,000)
GREATER GLASGOW (1:150,000)
EDINBURGH & THE LOTHIANS (1:150,000)
ISLE OF ARRAN (1:63,360)
FIFE (1:100,000)
LOCH LOMOND & TROSSACHS (1:150,000)
ARGYLL & LOCH LOMOND (1:275,000)
PERTHSHIRE (1:150,000)
FORT WILLIAM, BEN NEVIS, GLEN COE (1:185,000)
IONA (1:10,000) & MULL (1:115,000)
GRAMPIAN HIGHLANDS (1:185,000)
LOCH NESS & INVERNESS (1:150,000)
AVIEMORE & SPEY VALLEY (1:150,000)
SKYE & LOCHALSH (1:130,000)
ARGYLL & THE ISLES (1:200,000)
CAITHNESS & SUTHERLAND (1:185,000)
HIGHLANDS OF SCOTLAND (1:275,000)
WESTERN ISLES (1:125,000)
ORKNEY & SHETLAND (1:128,000)
ENGLAND & WALES (1:650,000)
SCOTLAND (1:500,000)
HISTORIC SCOTLAND (1:500,000)
SCOTLAND CLAN MAP (1:625,000)
BRITISH ISLES (1:1,100,000)
GREAT BRITAIN (1:1,100,000)

COUNTY ATLASES

BEDFORDSHIRE
BERKSHIRE
BUCKINGHAMSHIRE
CAMBRIDGESHIRE
CHESHIRE
CORNWALL
DERBYSHIRE
DEVON
DORSET
ESSEX
GLOUCESTERSHIRE
HAMPSHIRE
HERTFORDSHIRE
KENT
LEICESTERSHIRE
NORTHAMPTONSHIRE
NOTTINGHAMSHIRE
OXFORDSHIRE
SHROPSHIRE
SOMERSET
STAFFORDSHIRE
SURREY
SUSSEX (EAST)
SUSSEX (WEST)
WILTSHIRE

OTHER MAPS

KENT TO CORNWALL (1:460,000)
COUNTY MAP — DORSET
         — HAMPSHIRE
         — SOMERSET
         — WILTSHIRE
SOUTH EAST ASIA (1:6,000,000)
CHINA (1:6,000,000)
NEPAL (1:800,000)

STREET PLANS

BODMIN & WADEBRIDGE
CAMBORNE & REDRUTH
EDINBURGH TOURIST PLAN
NEWQUAY
PENZANCE & ST. IVES
ST. ALBANS
ST. AUSTELL

EUROPEAN LEISURE MAPS

EUROPE (1:3,100,000)
BENELUX (1:600,000)
FRANCE (1:1,000,000)
GERMANY (1:1,000,000)
IRELAND (1:625,000)
ITALY (1:1,000,000)
SCANDINAVIA (1:2,600,000)
SPAIN & PORTUGAL (1:100,000)
CROSS CHANNEL VISITORS' MAP (1:530,000)
WORLD (1:35,000,000)
WORLD FLAT

NORTH FRENCH TOWNS ATLAS
BOULOGNE SHOPPERS MAP
CALAIS SHOPPERS MAP
DIEPPE SHOPPERS MAP

ESTATE PUBLICATIONS are also
Distributors in the U.K. for:
INTERNATIONAL TRAVEL MAPS, Canada

Catalogue and prices from ESTATE PUBLICATIONS,
Bridewell House, Tenterden, Kent. TN30 6EP
Tel: 01580 764225   Fax: 01580 763720